MY FIRST GIANT TRACING WORKBOOK

ABC

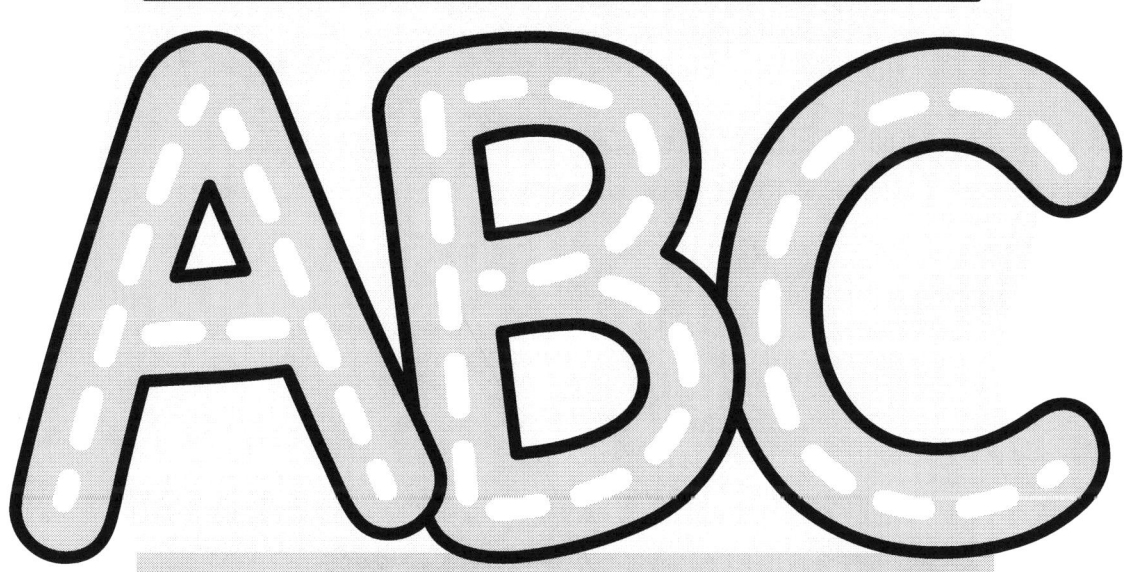

100+ LARGE FORMAT LETTERS, NUMBERS, AND SHAPES TO TRACE!

This book belongs to:

Scan this code for

FREE GOODIES!

Questions & Customer Service:
Email us at modernkidpress@gmailcom!

My First Giant Tracing Workbook
©Modern Kid Press. All rights reserved. No part of this publication may be reproduced, distributed, or transmitted, in any form or by any means, including photocopying, recording, or other electronic or mechanical methods, without prior written permission of the publisher, except in the case of brief quotations embodied in critical reviews and certain other noncommercial uses permitted by copyright law.

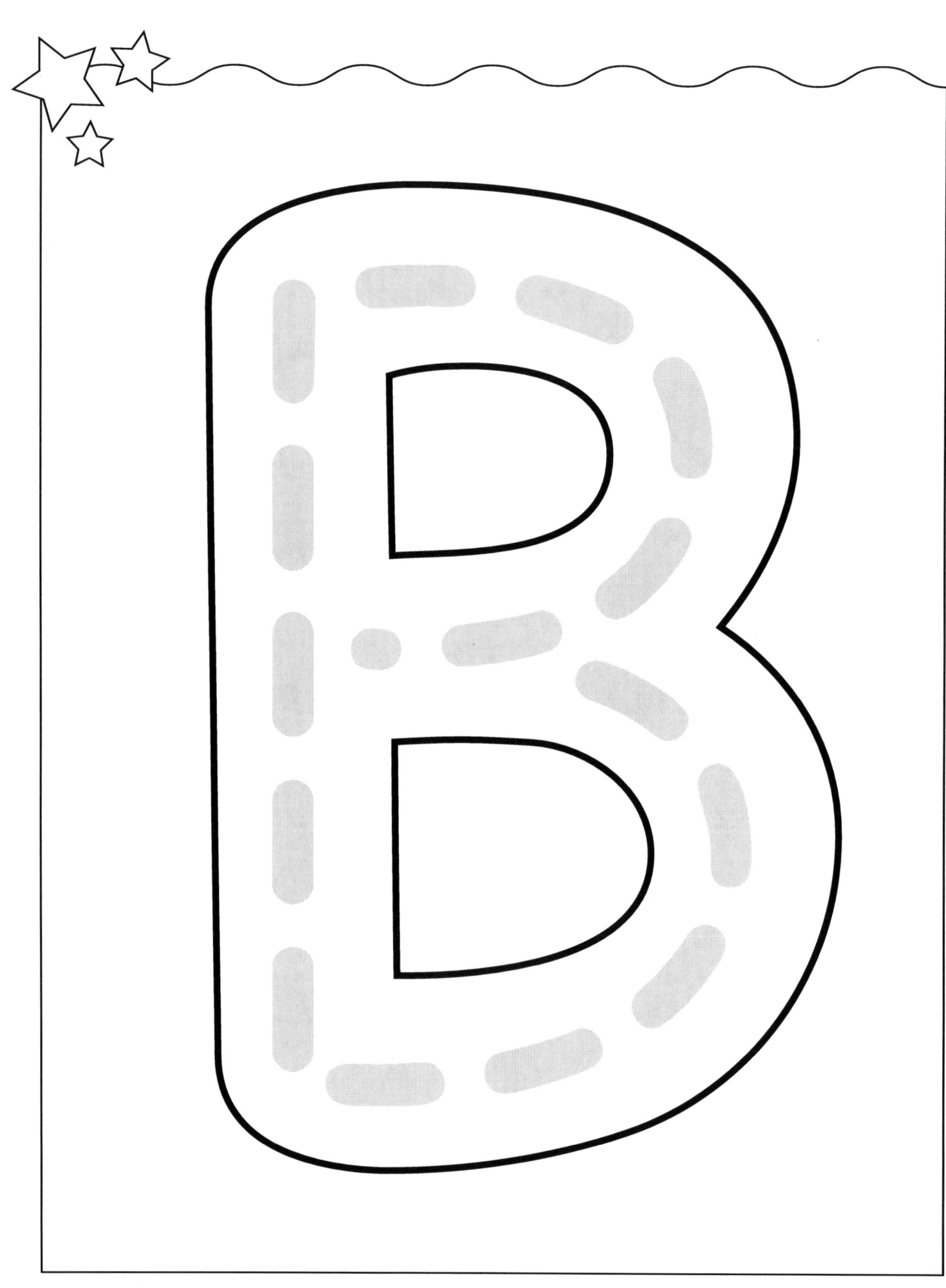

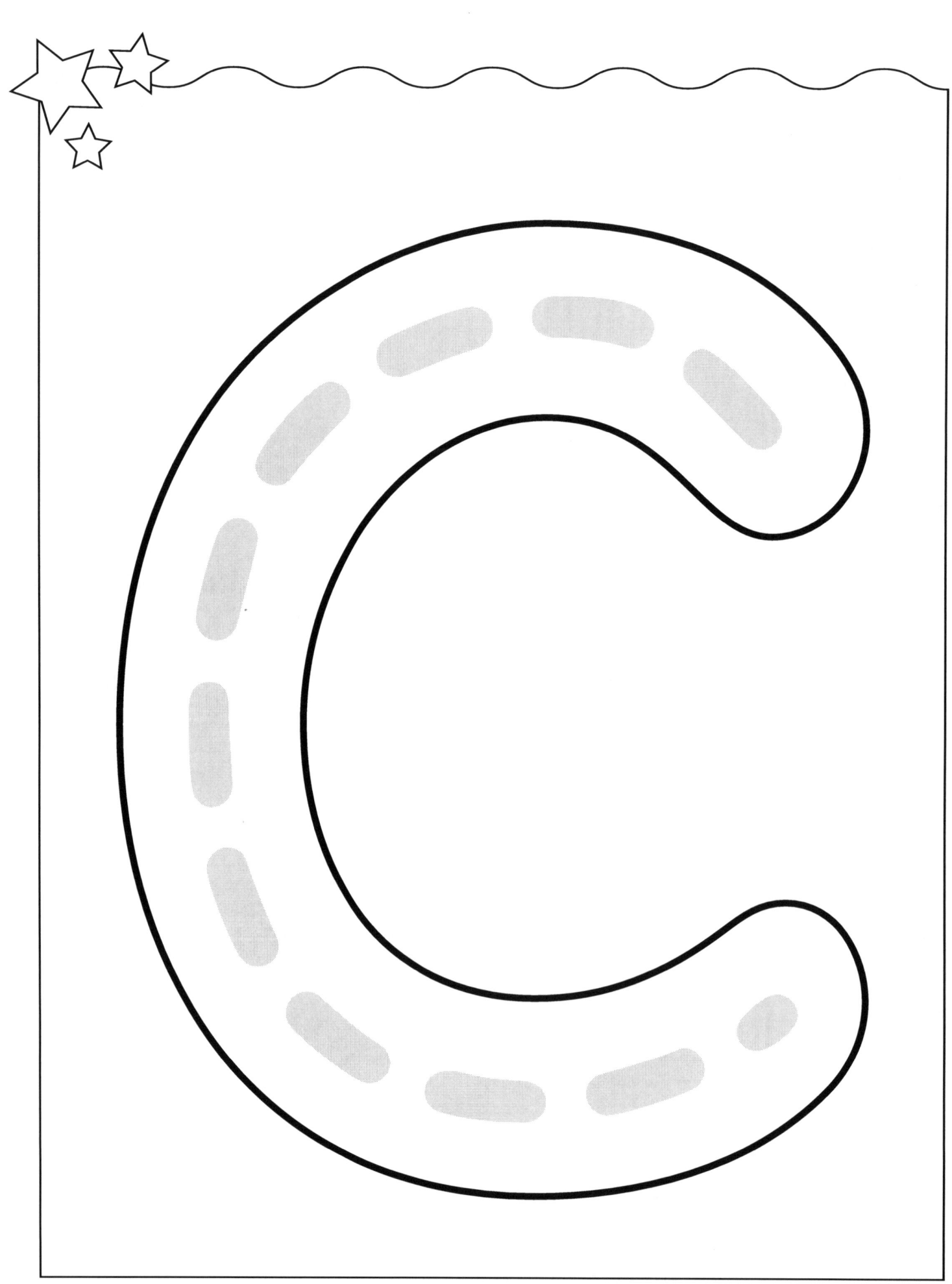

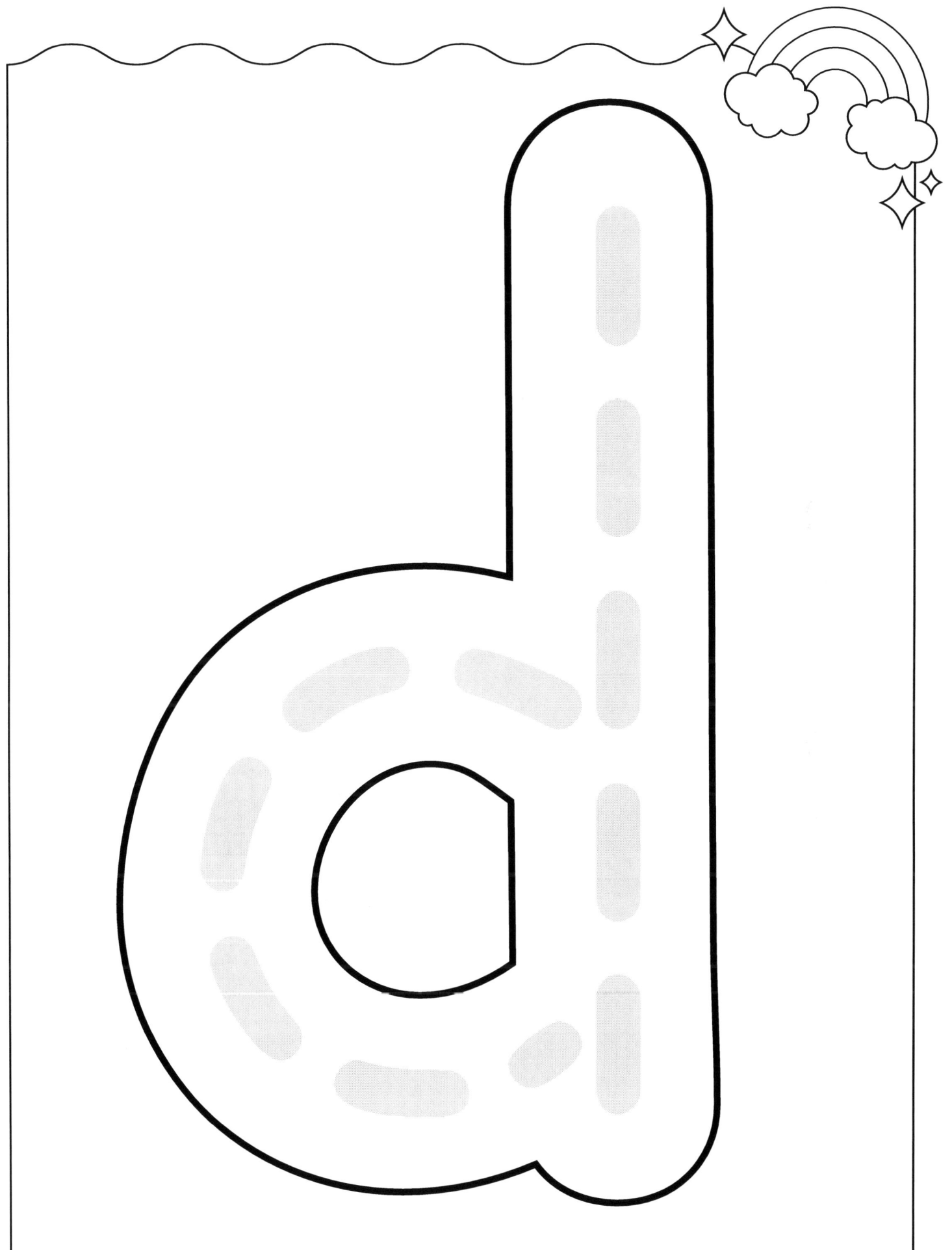

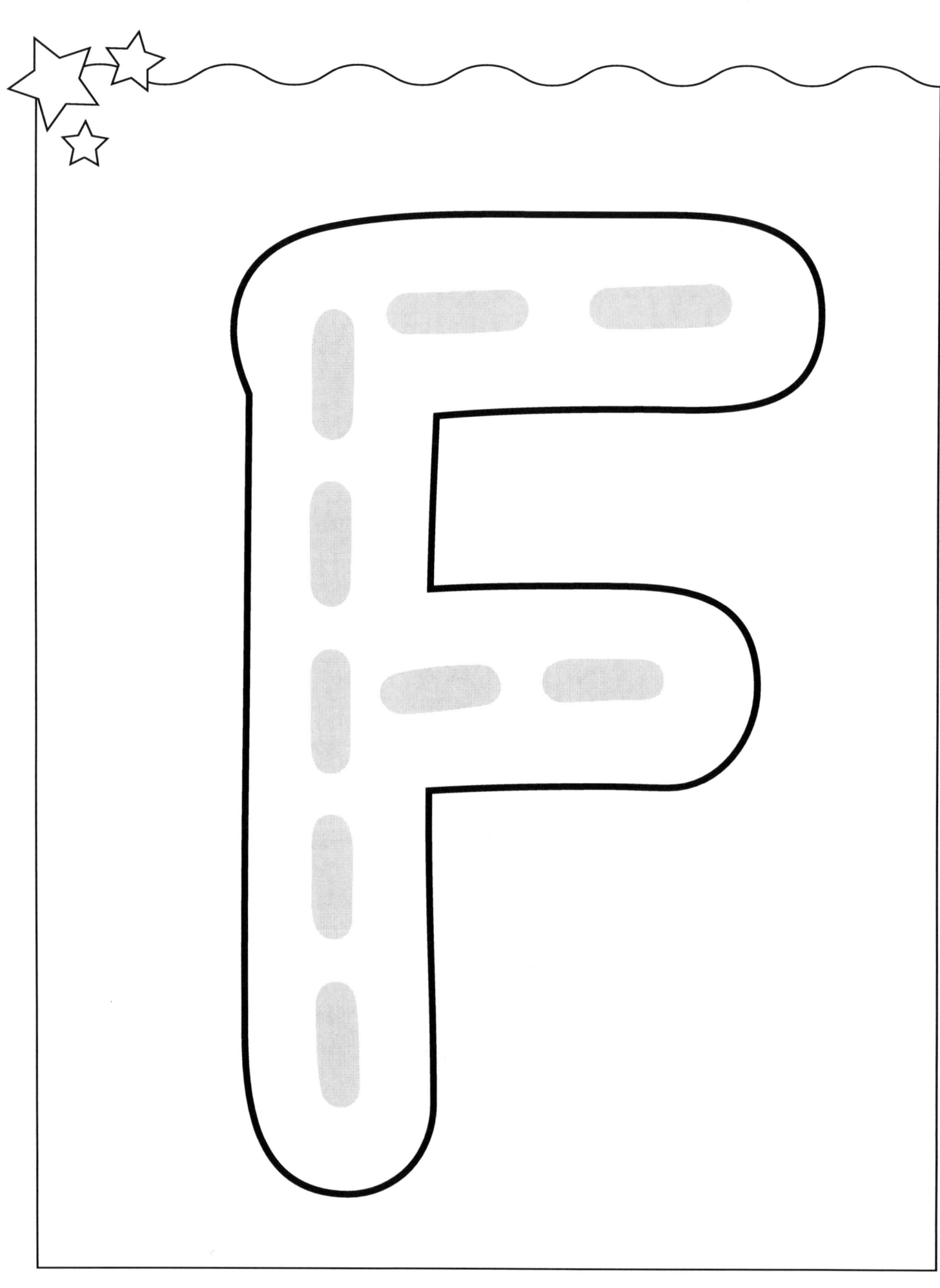

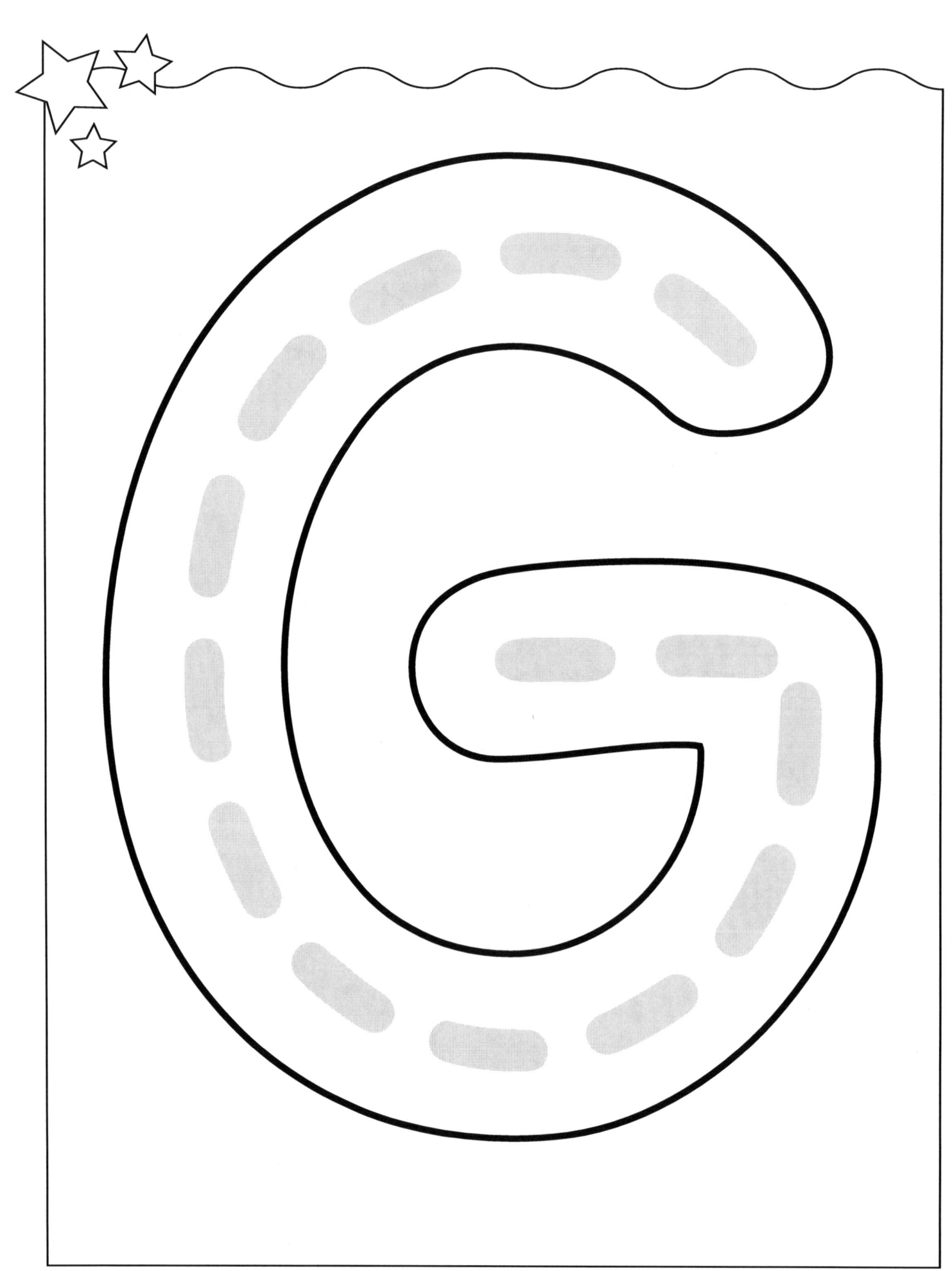

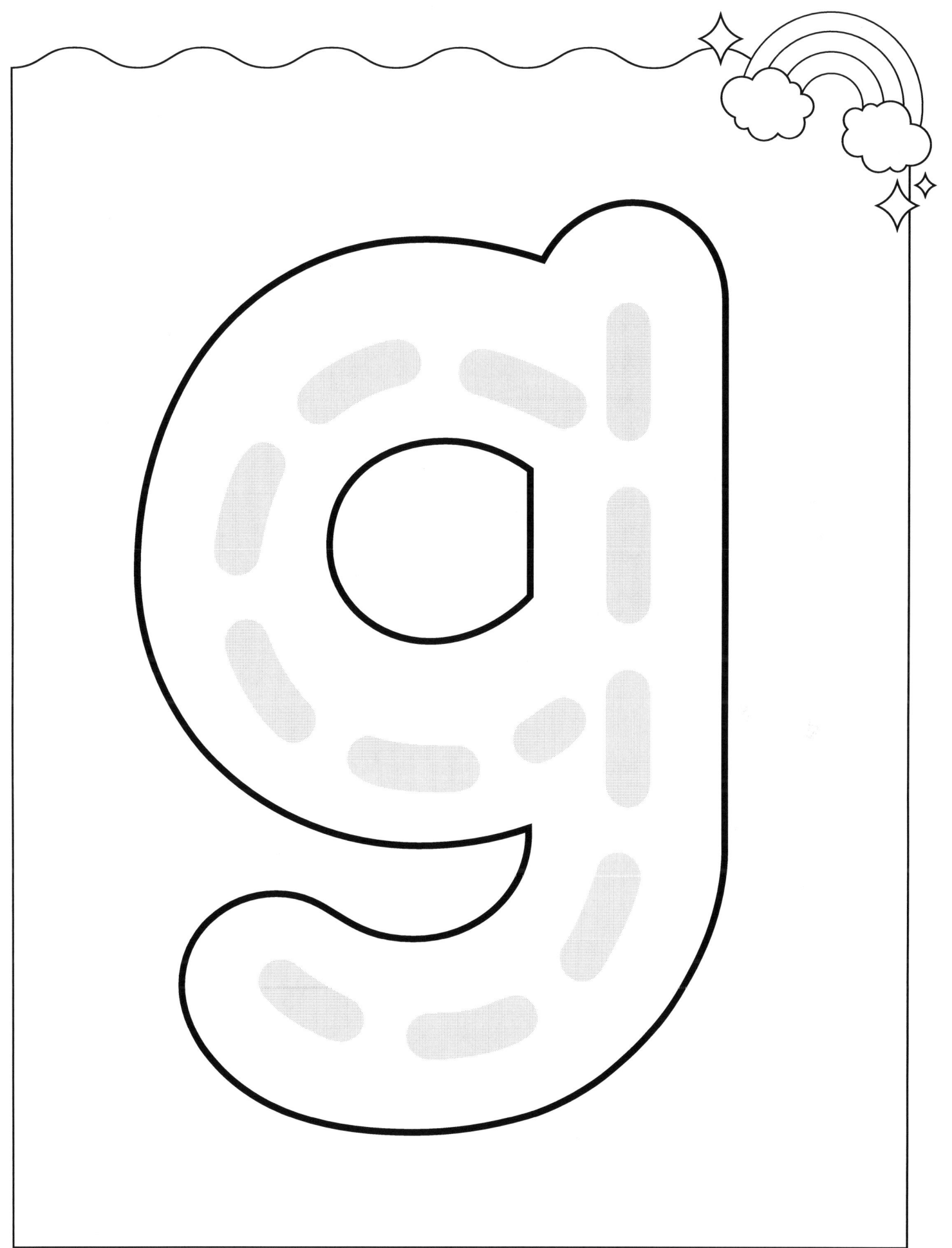

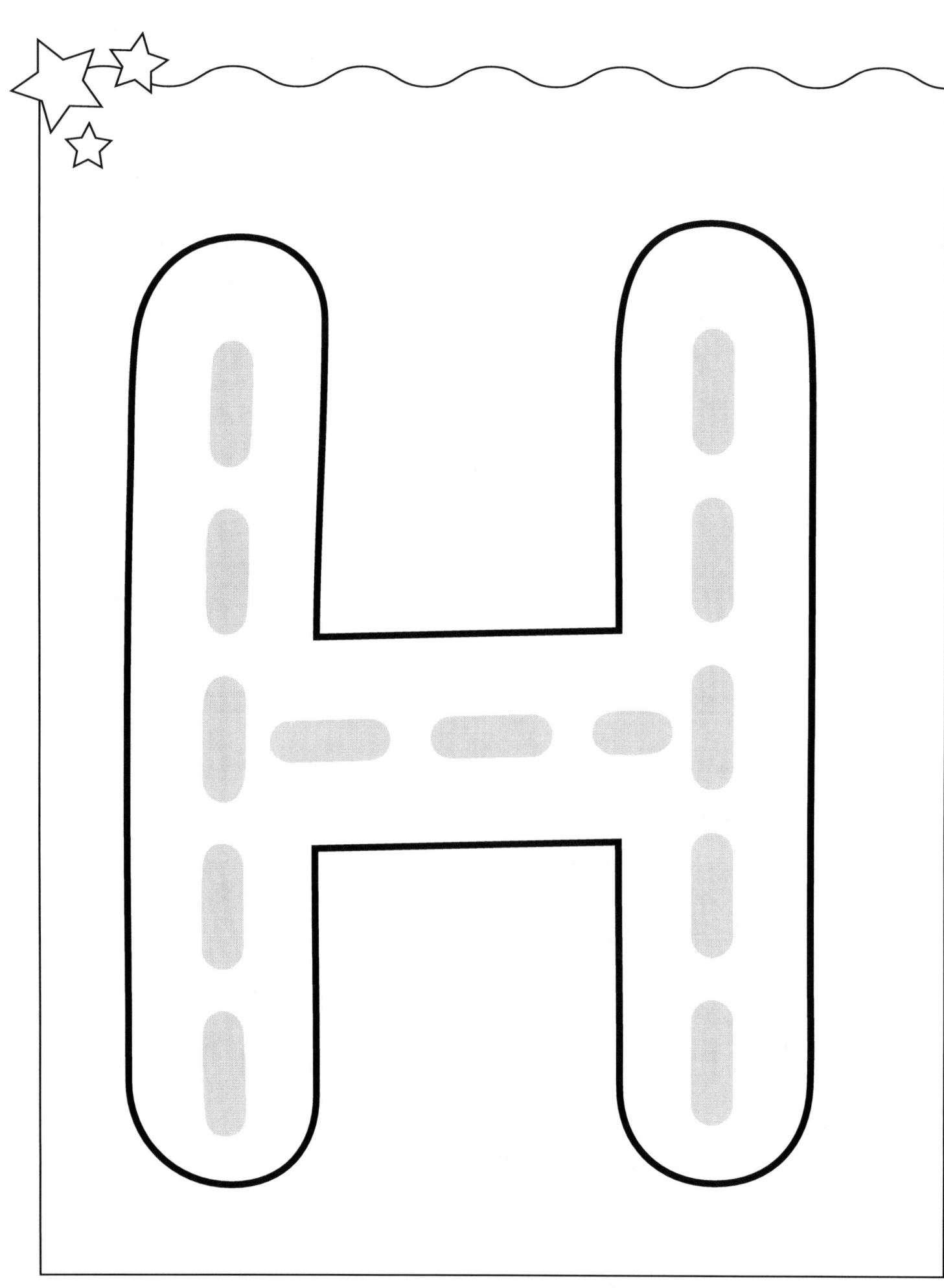

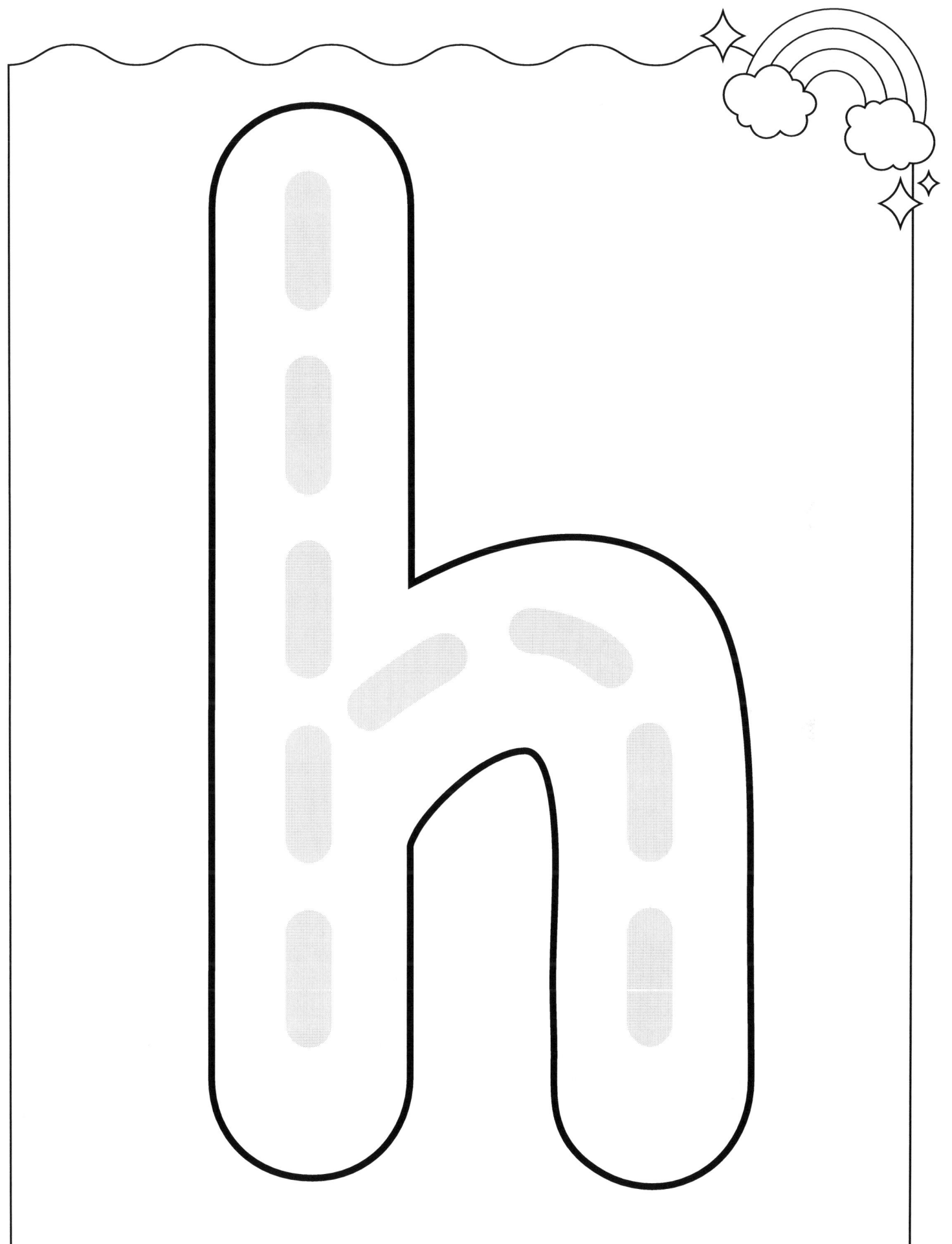

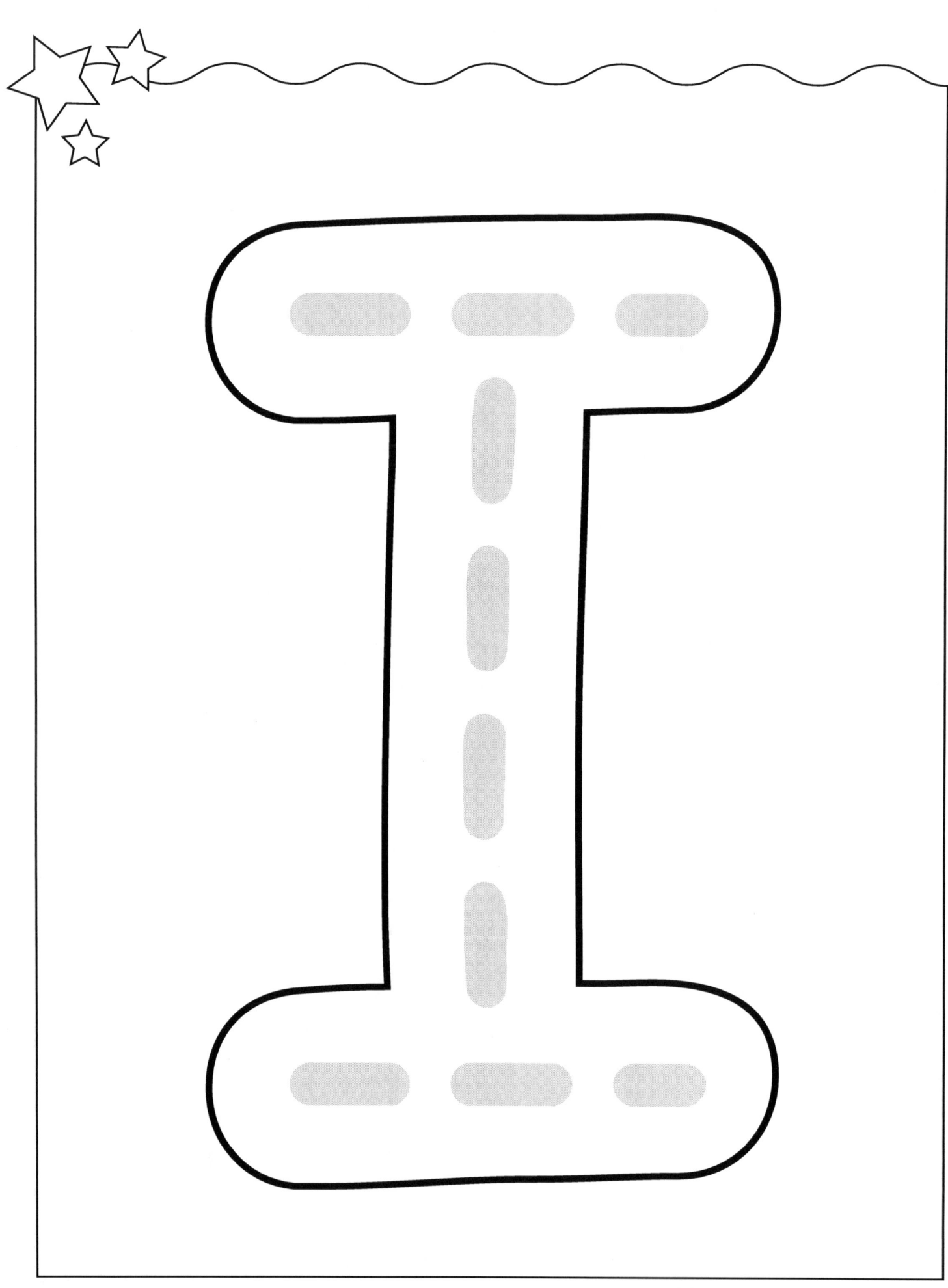

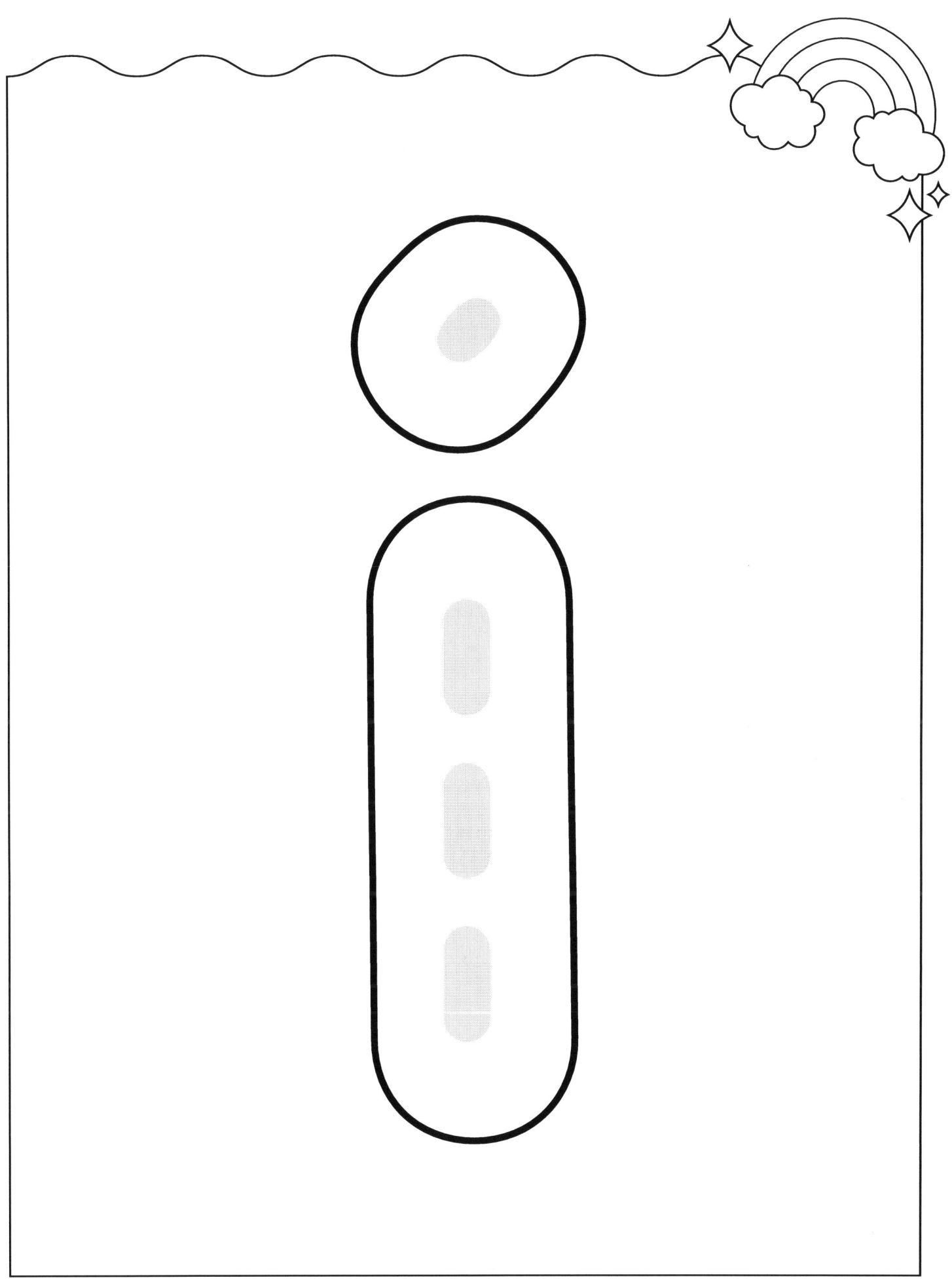

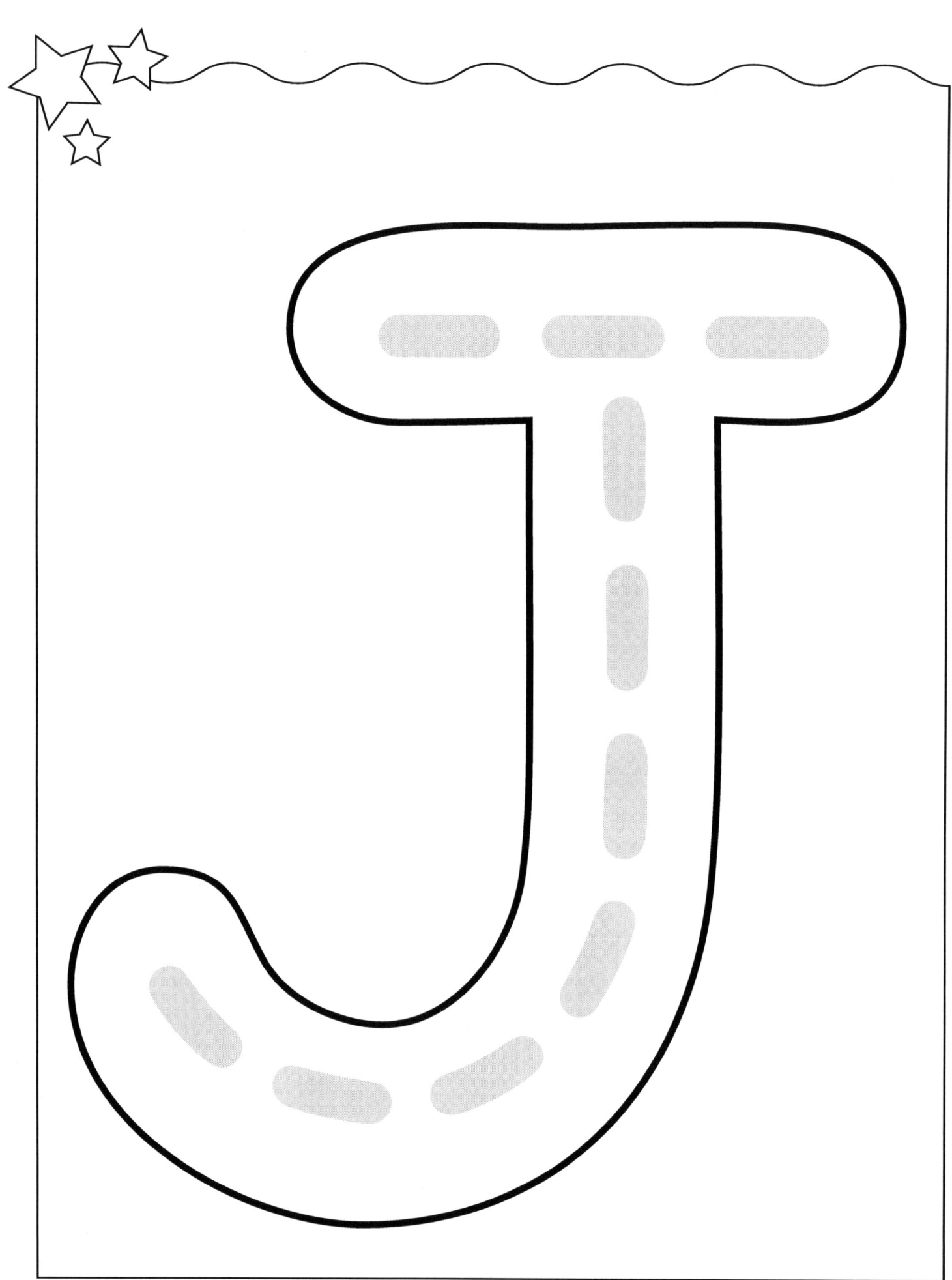

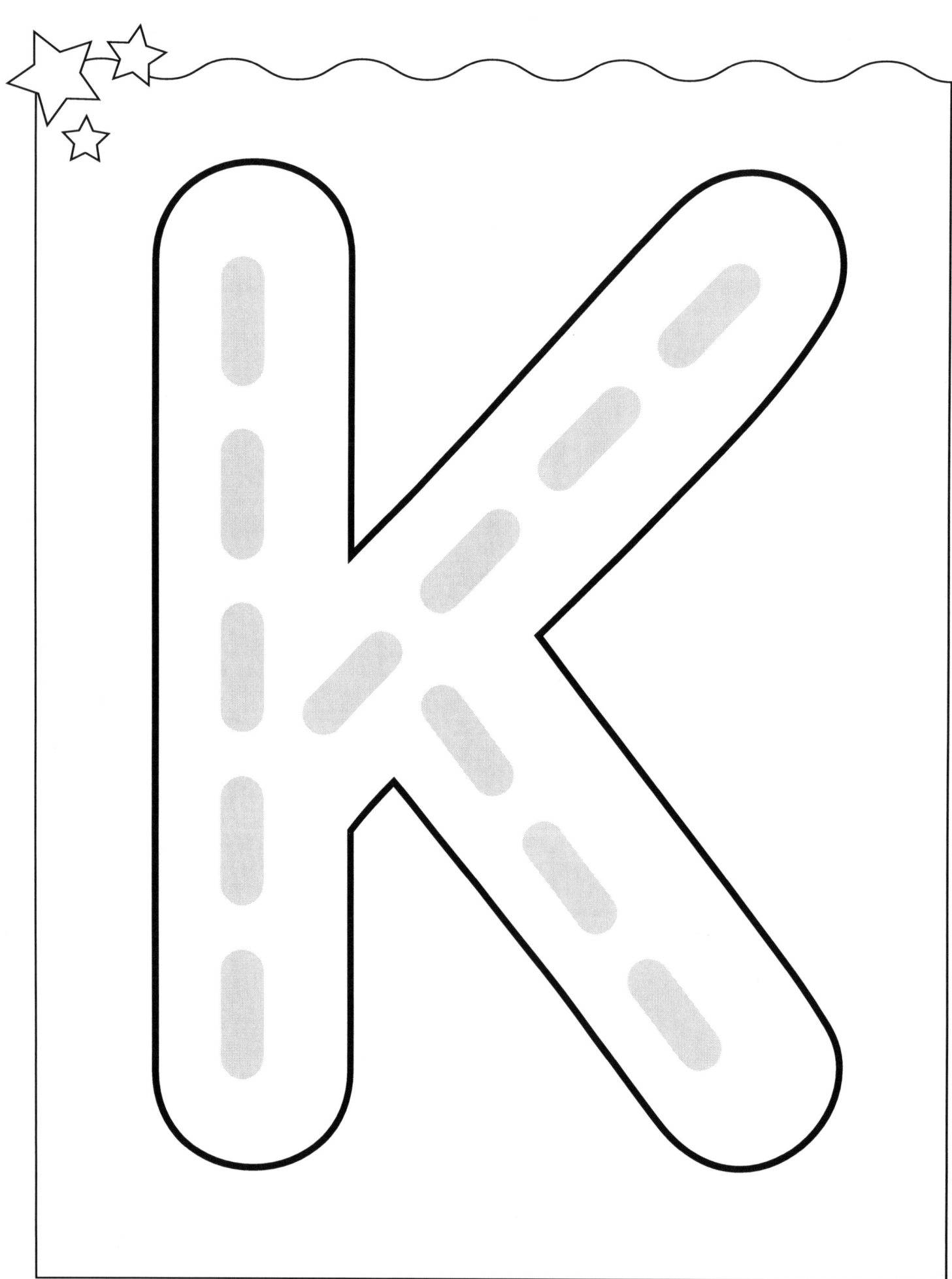

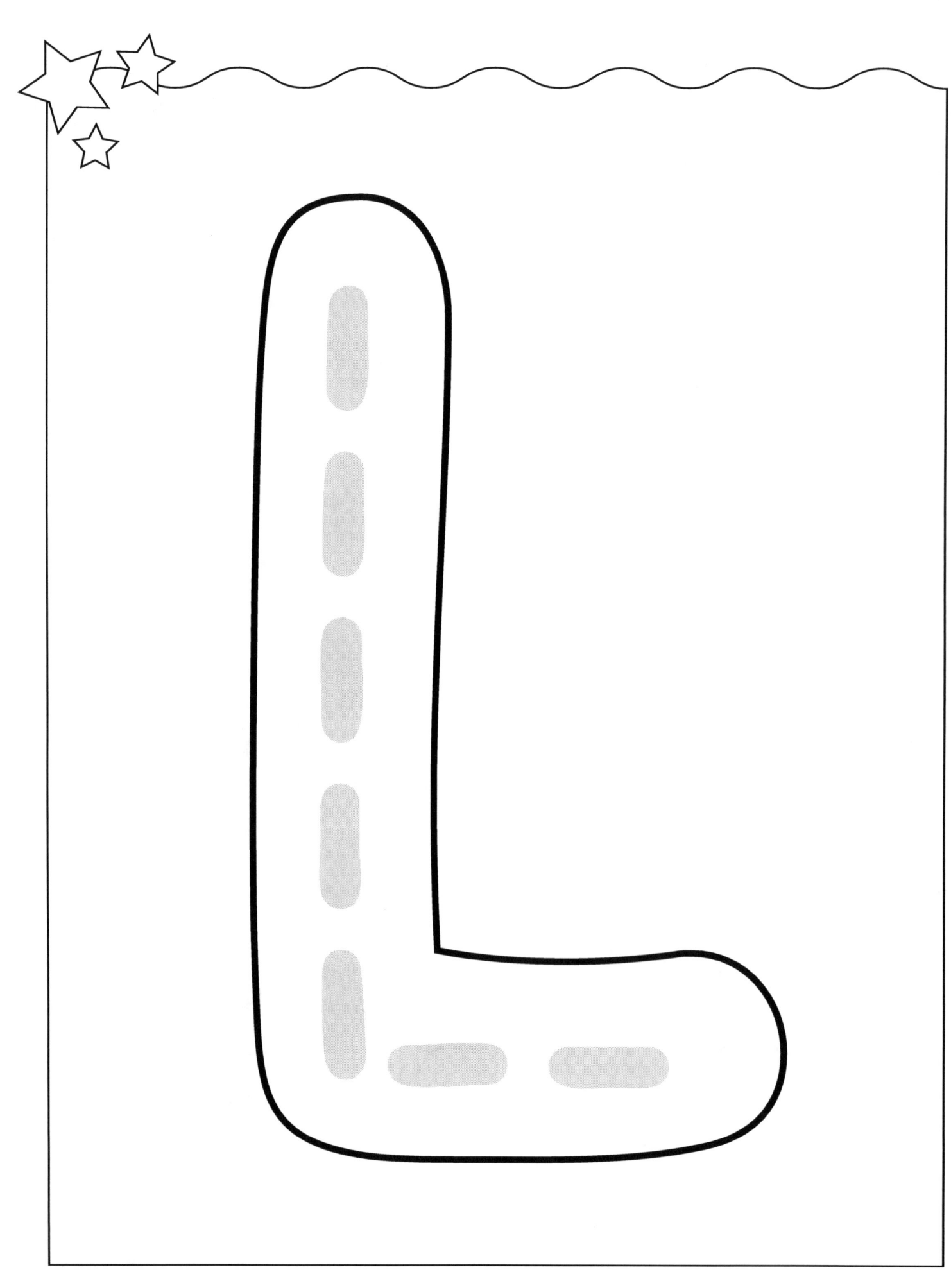

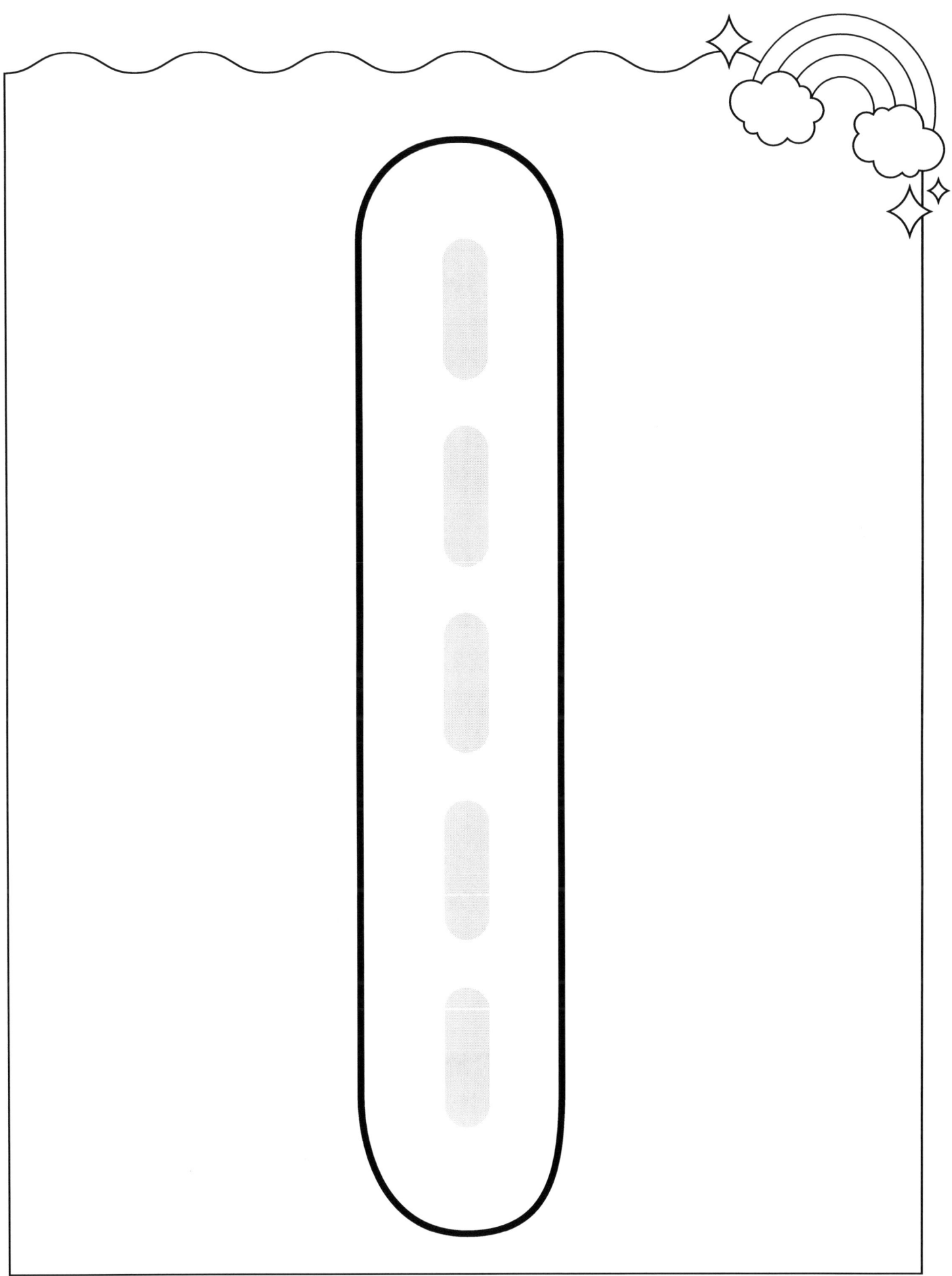

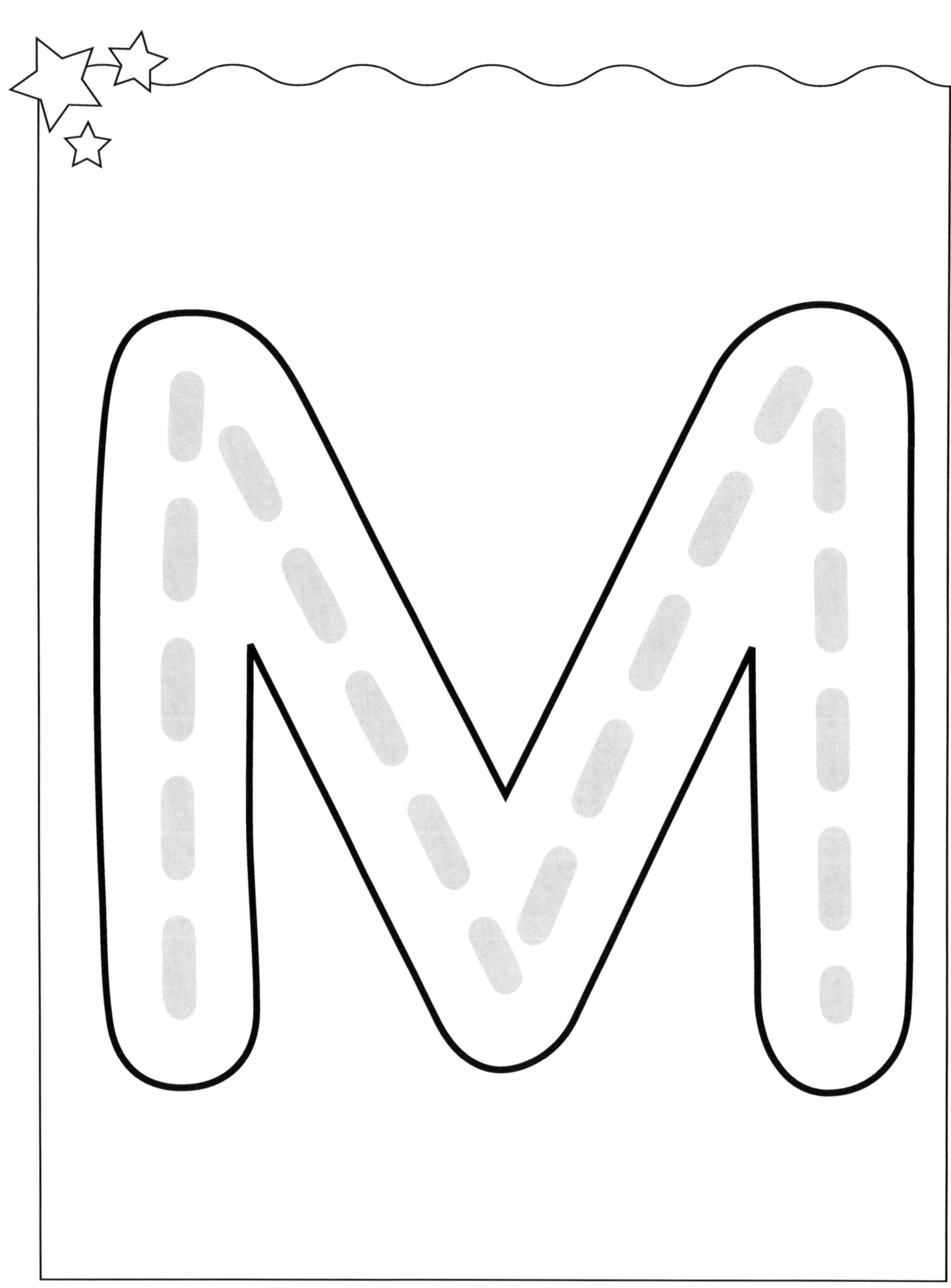

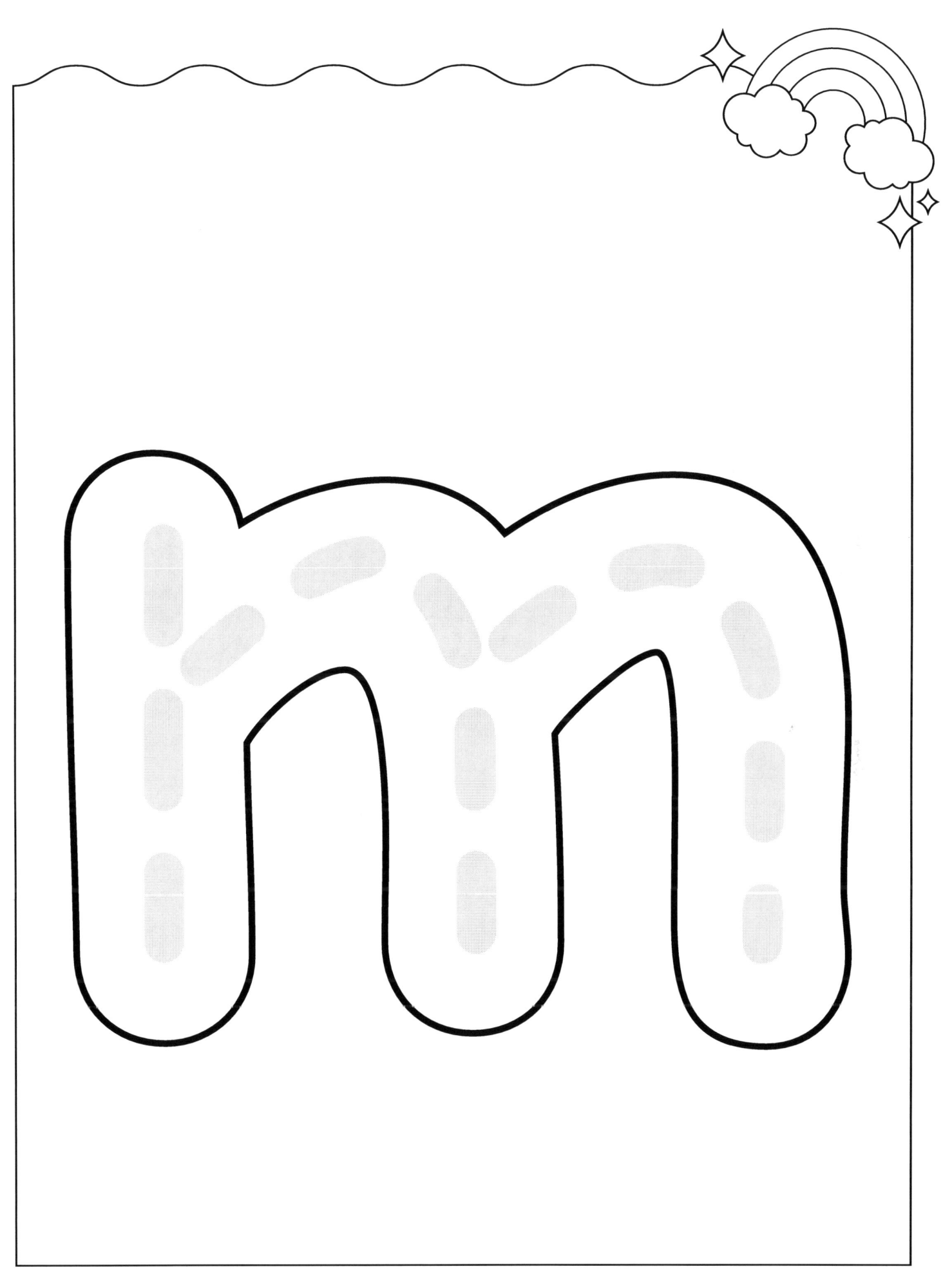

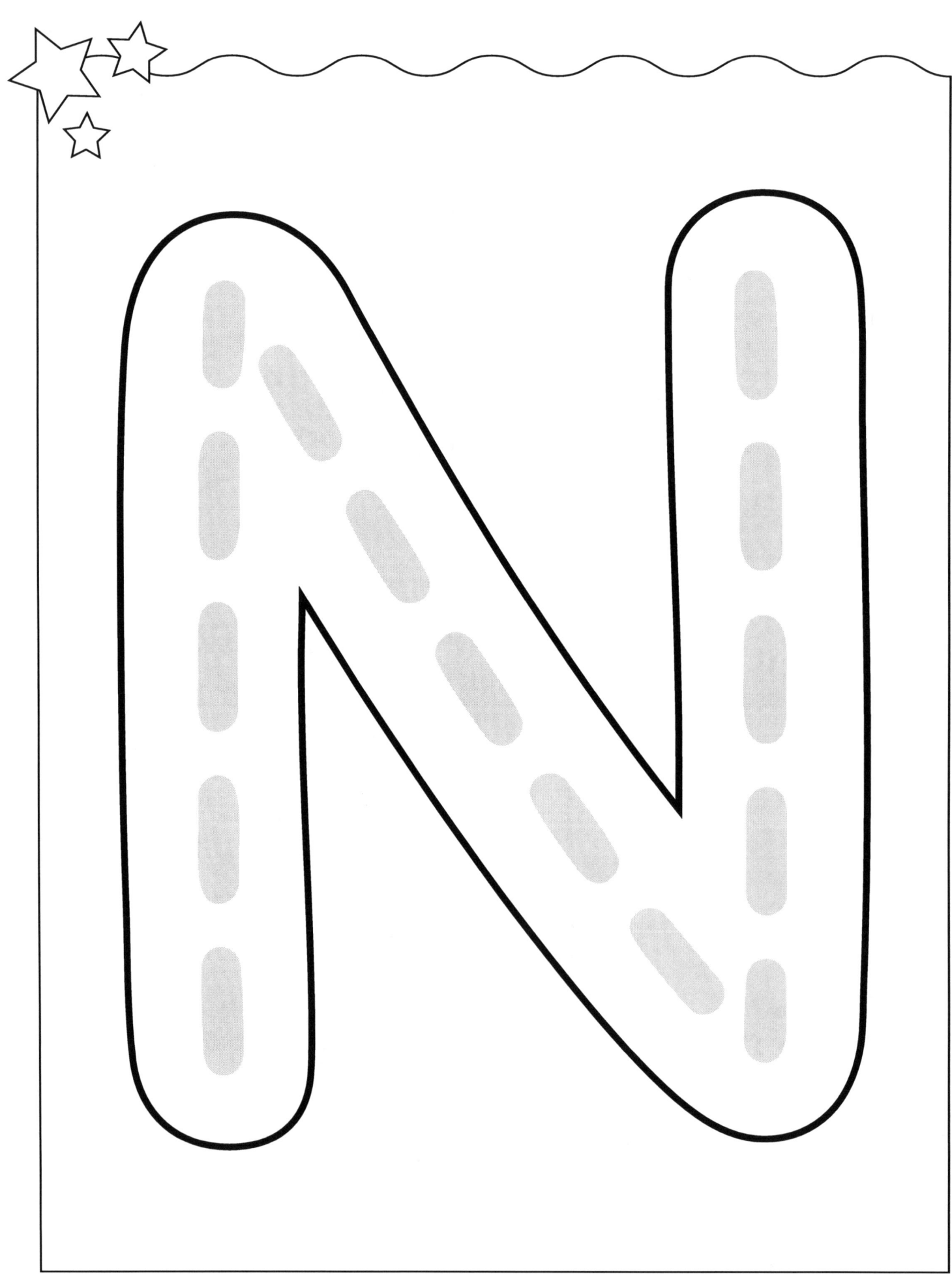

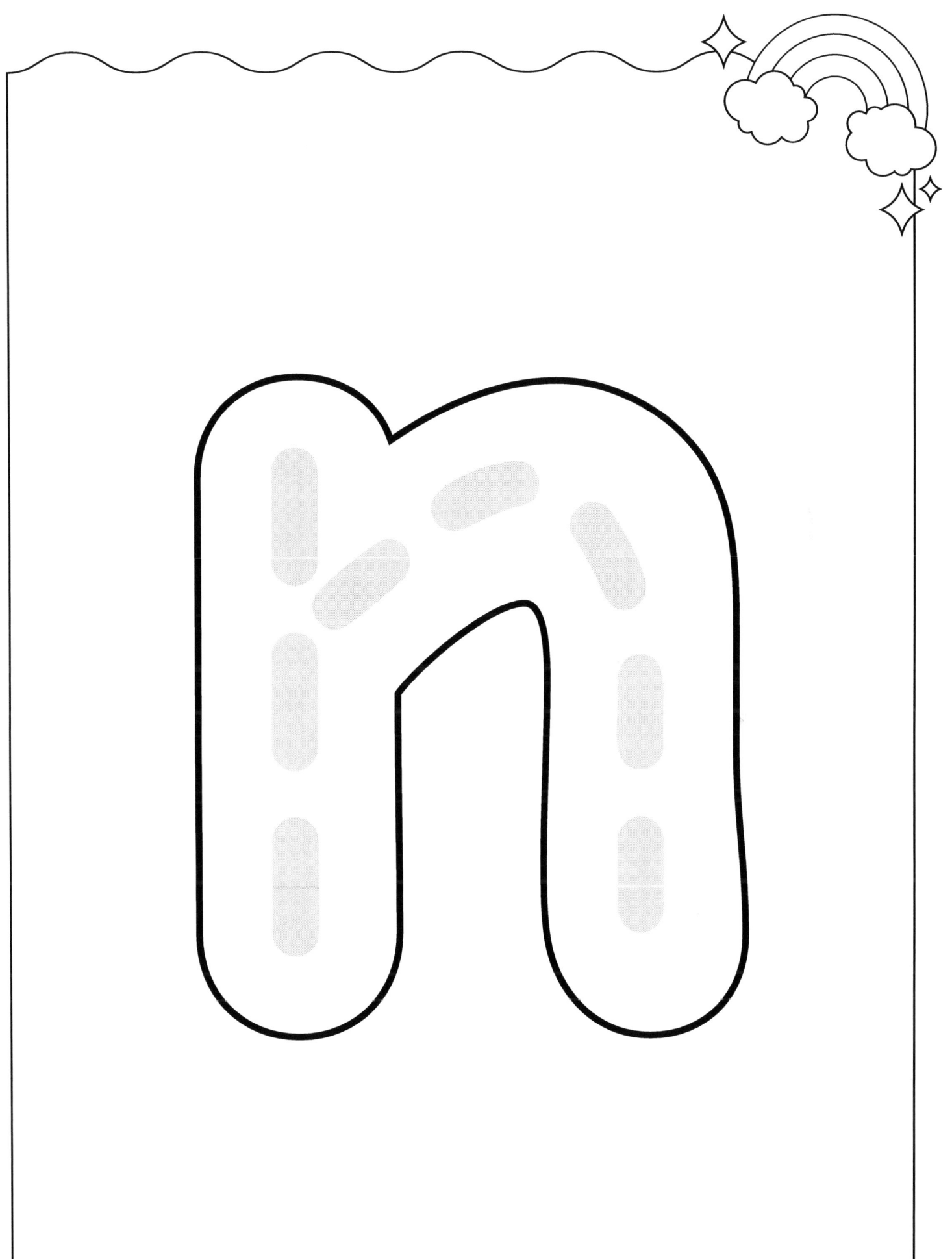

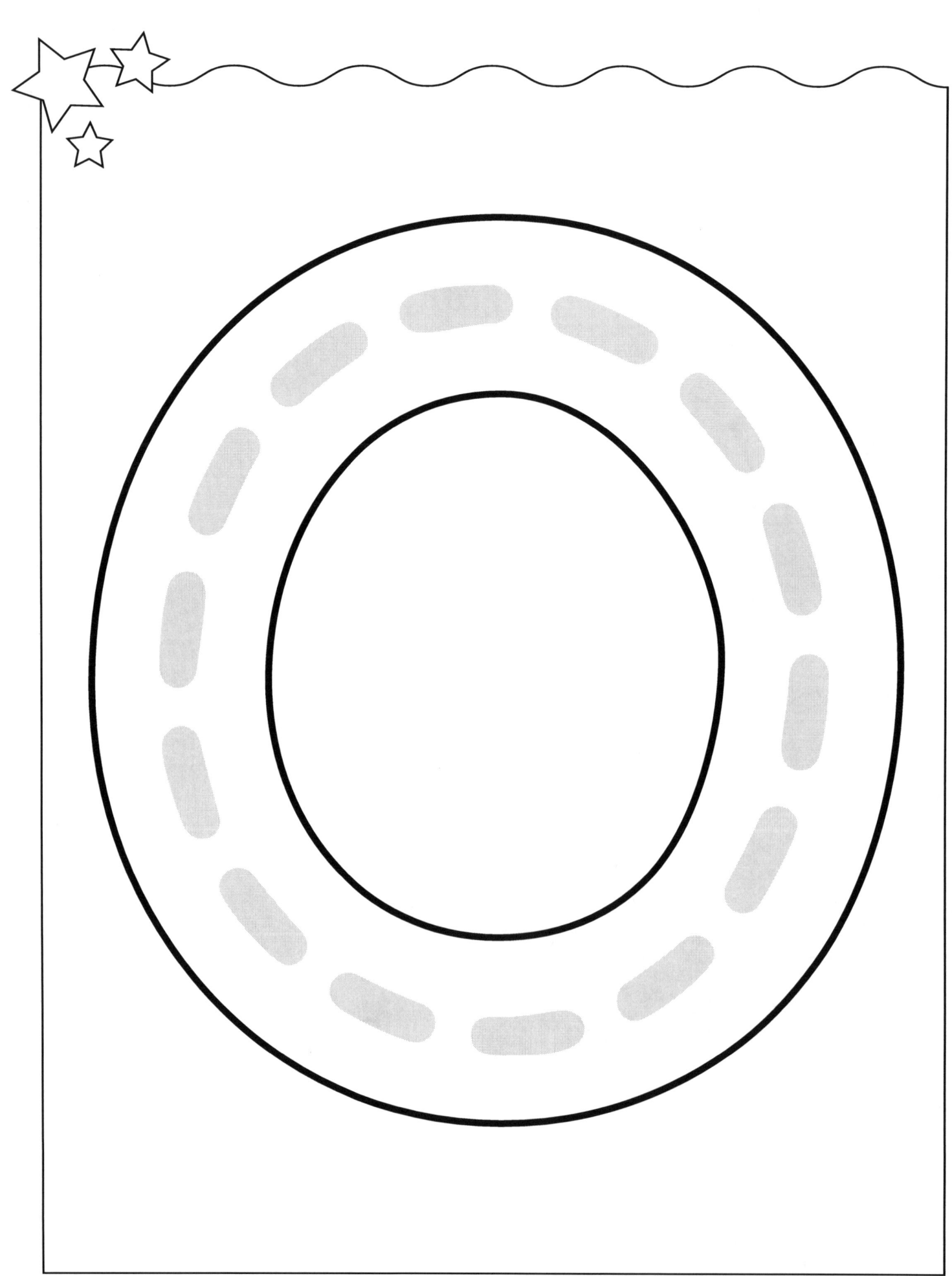

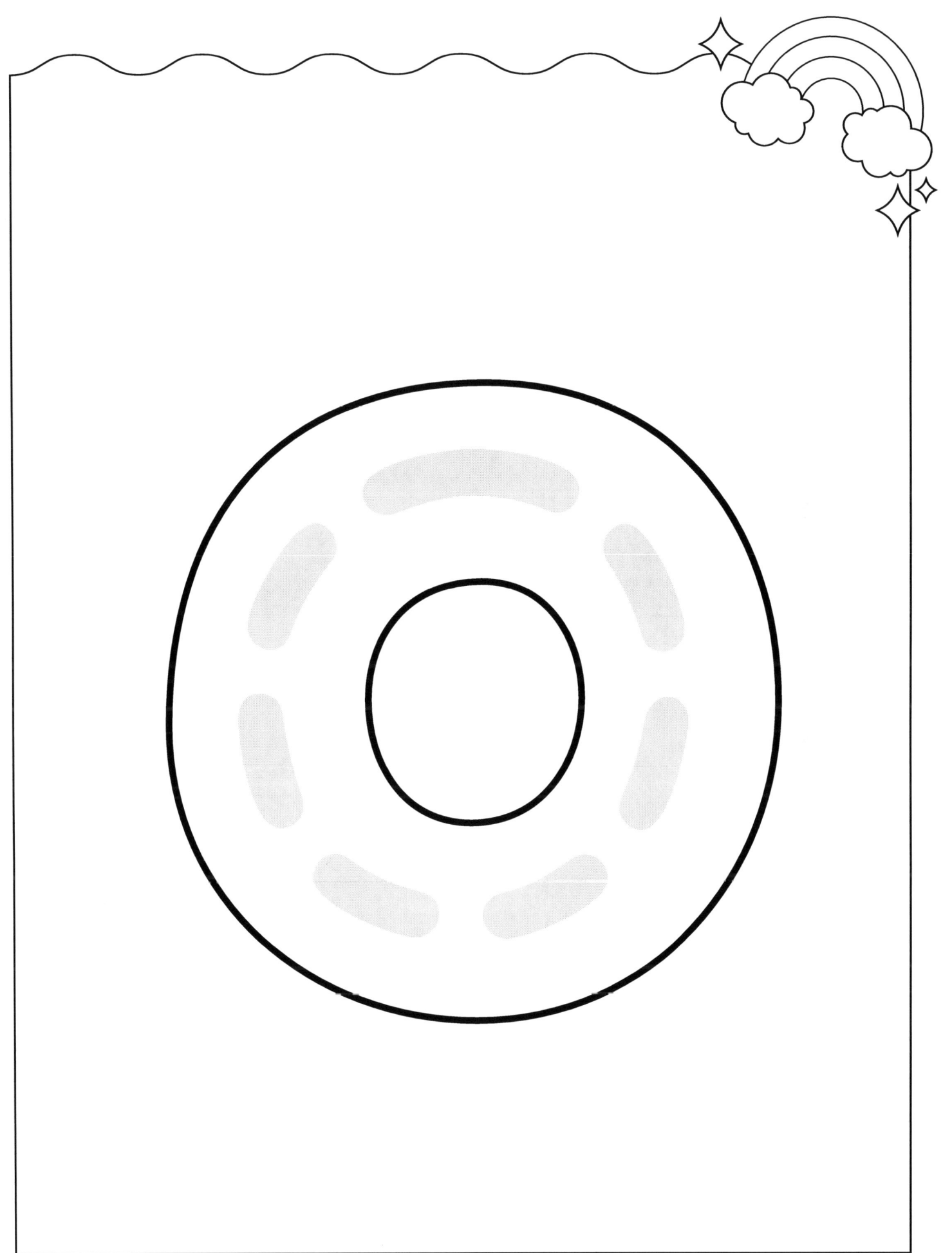

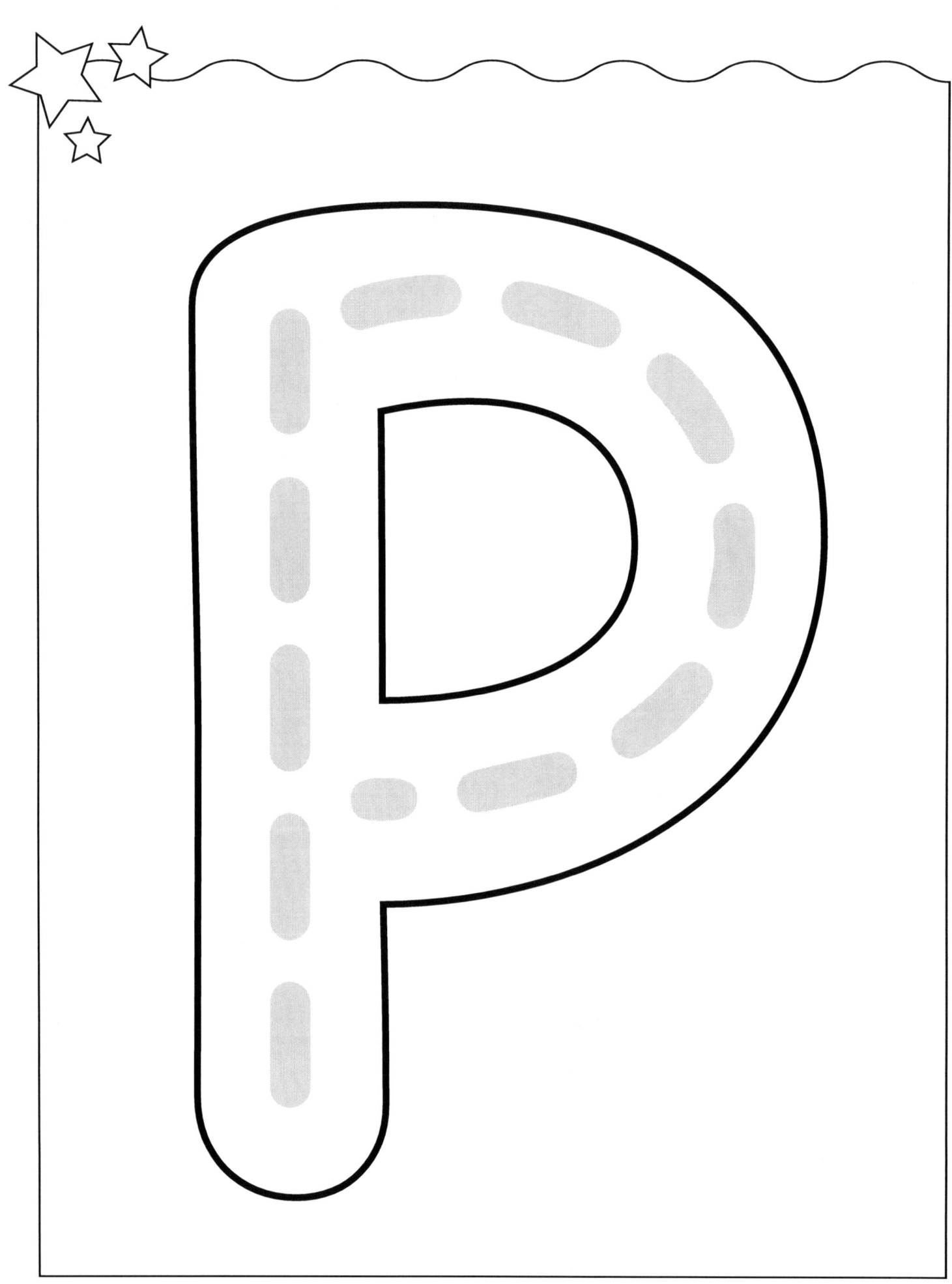

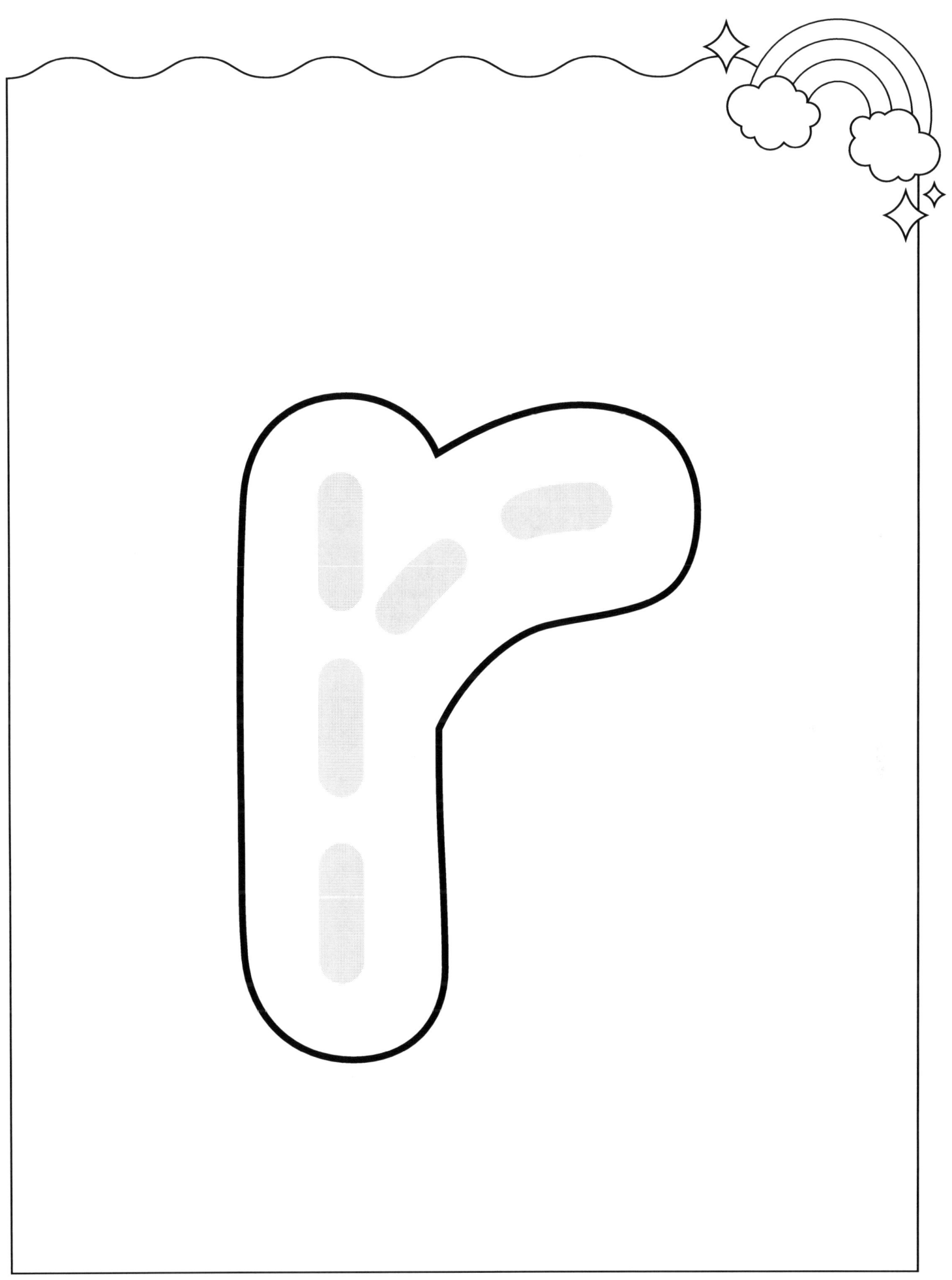

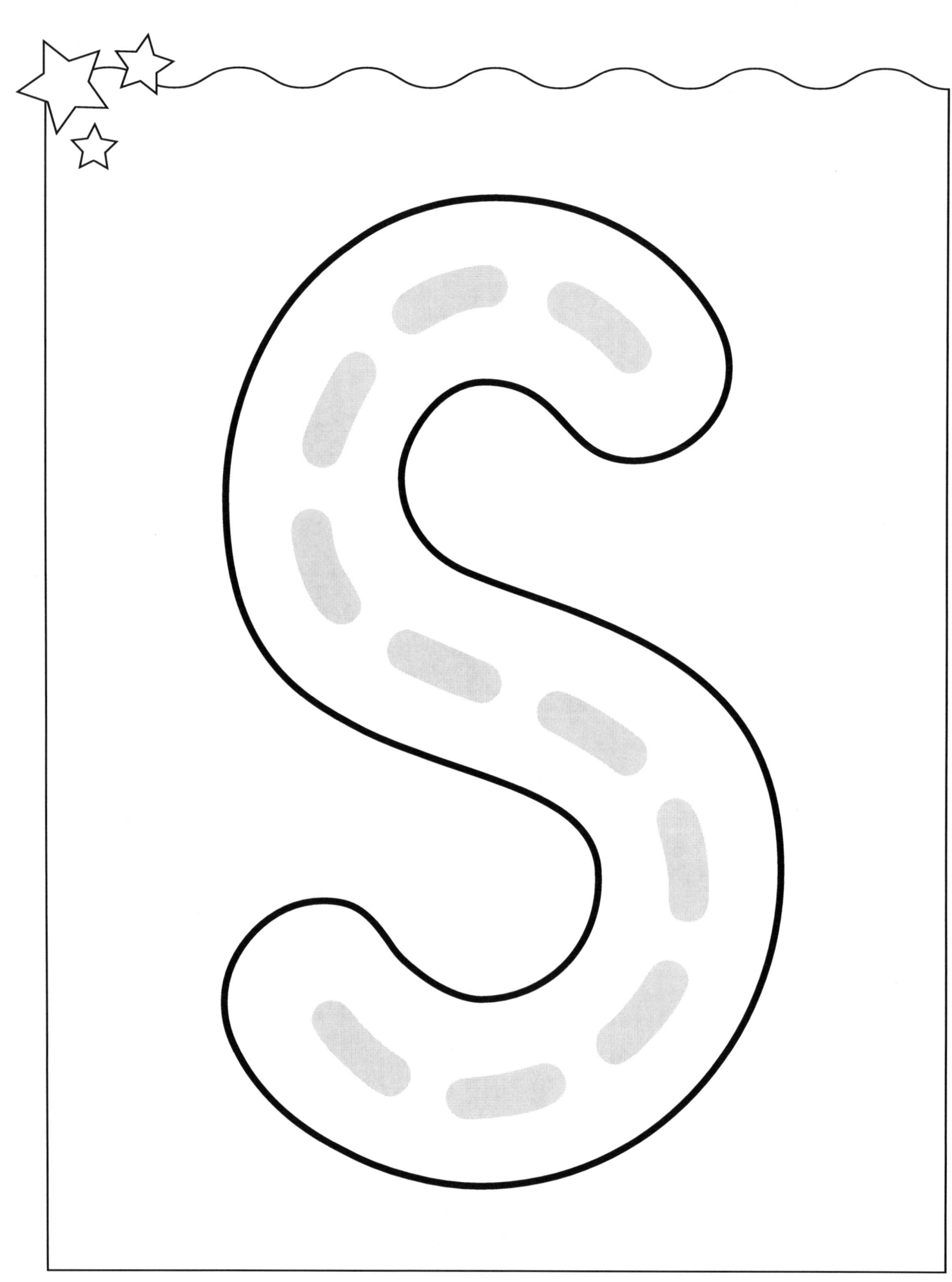

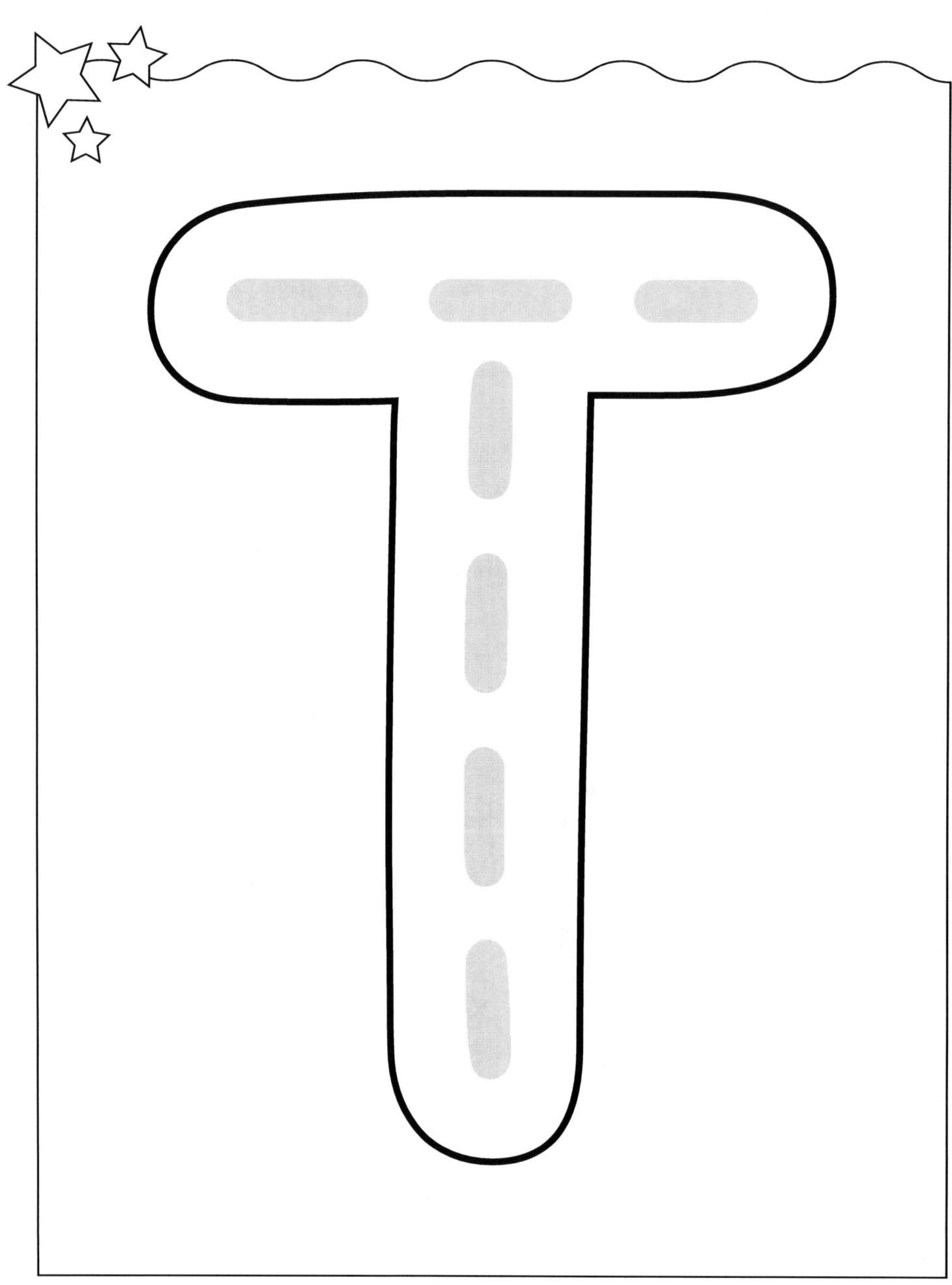

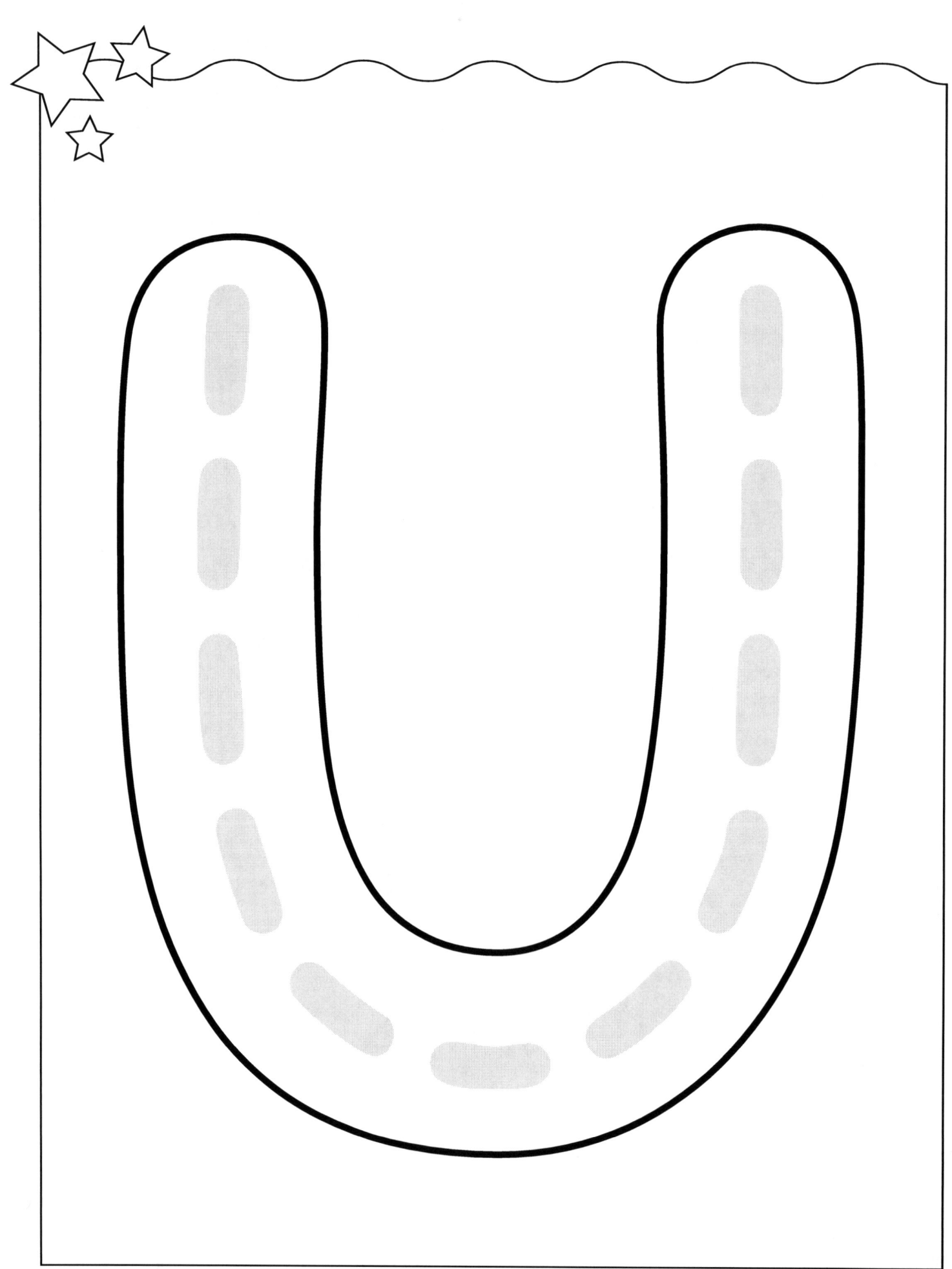

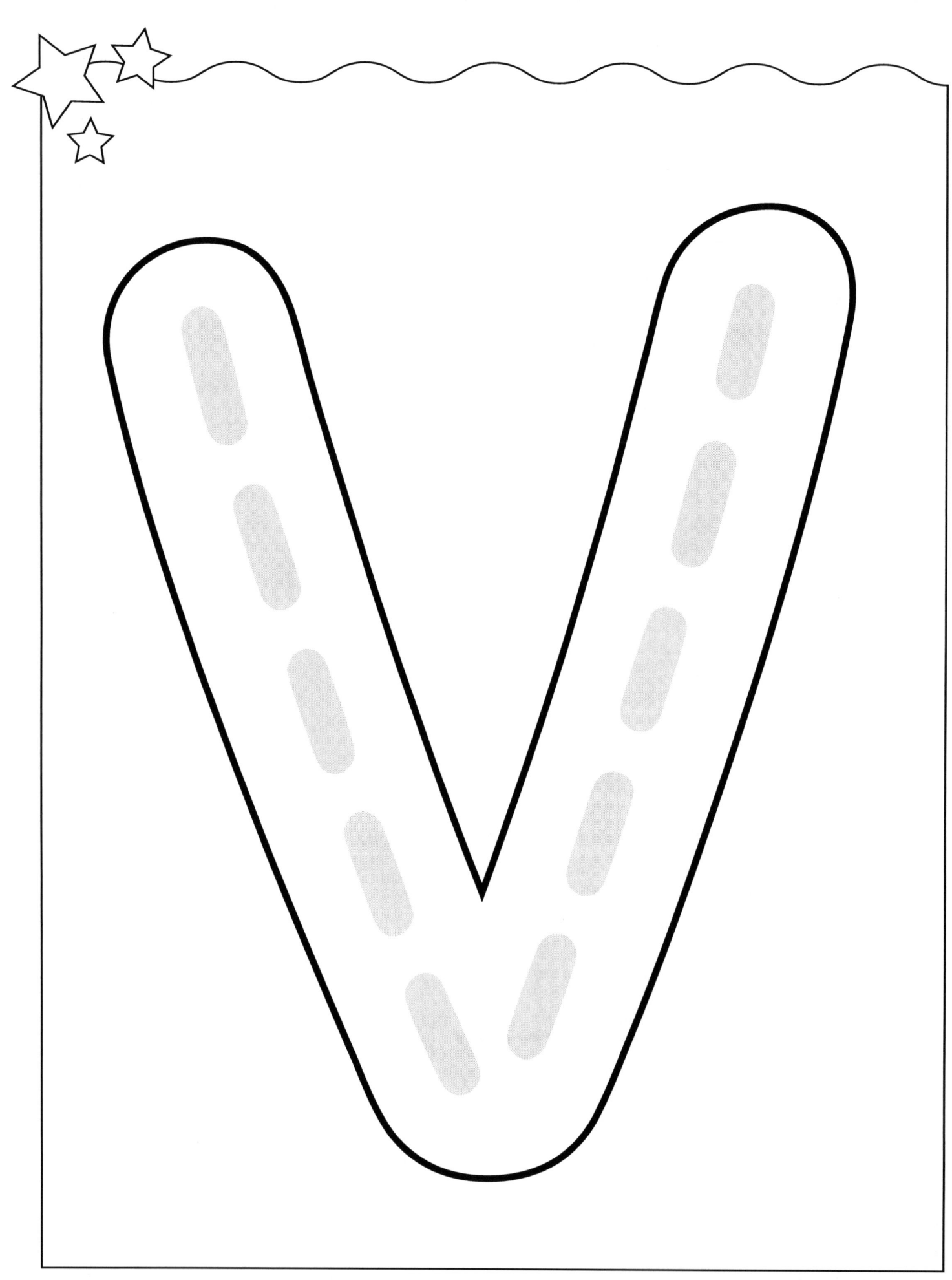

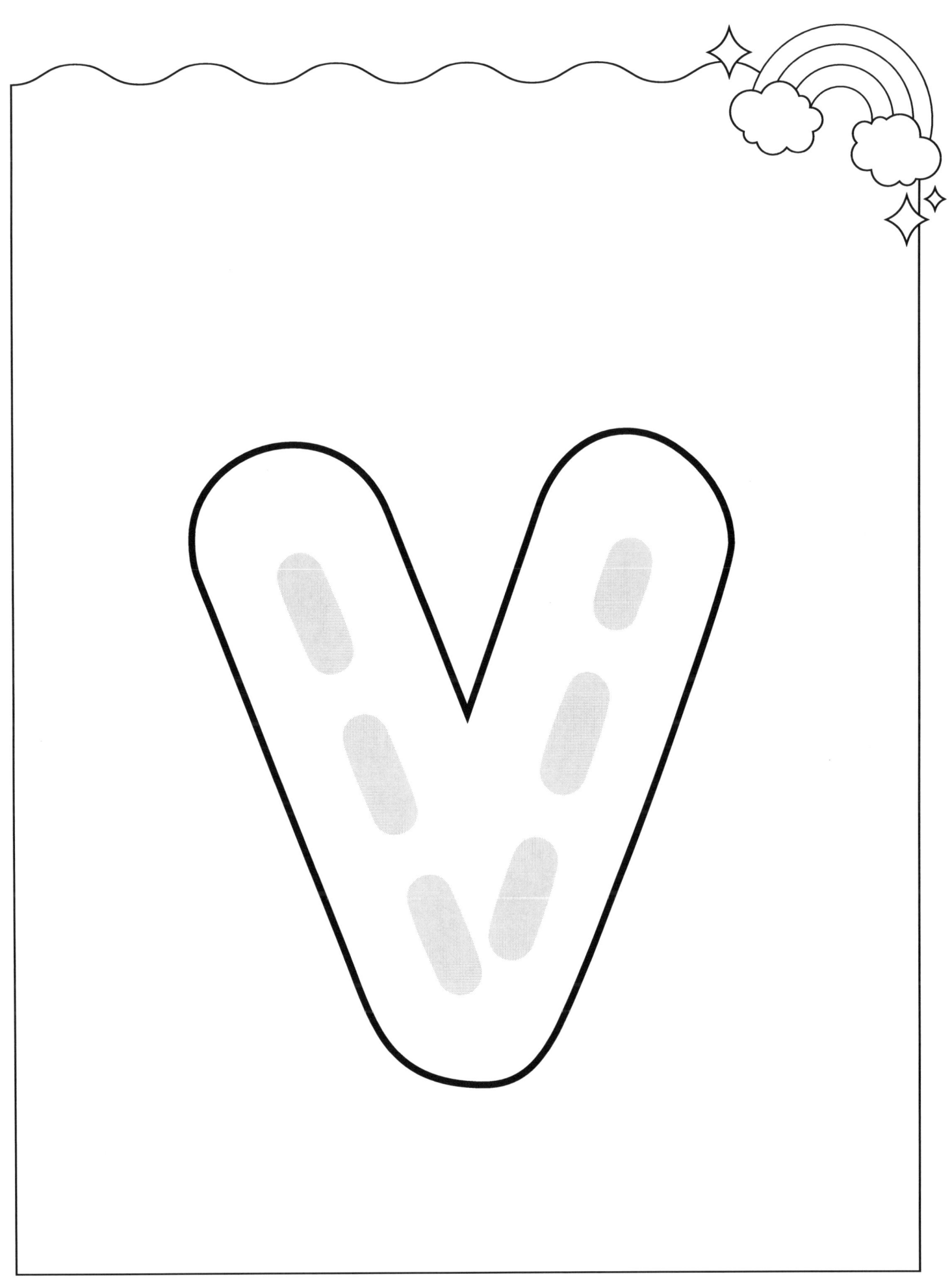

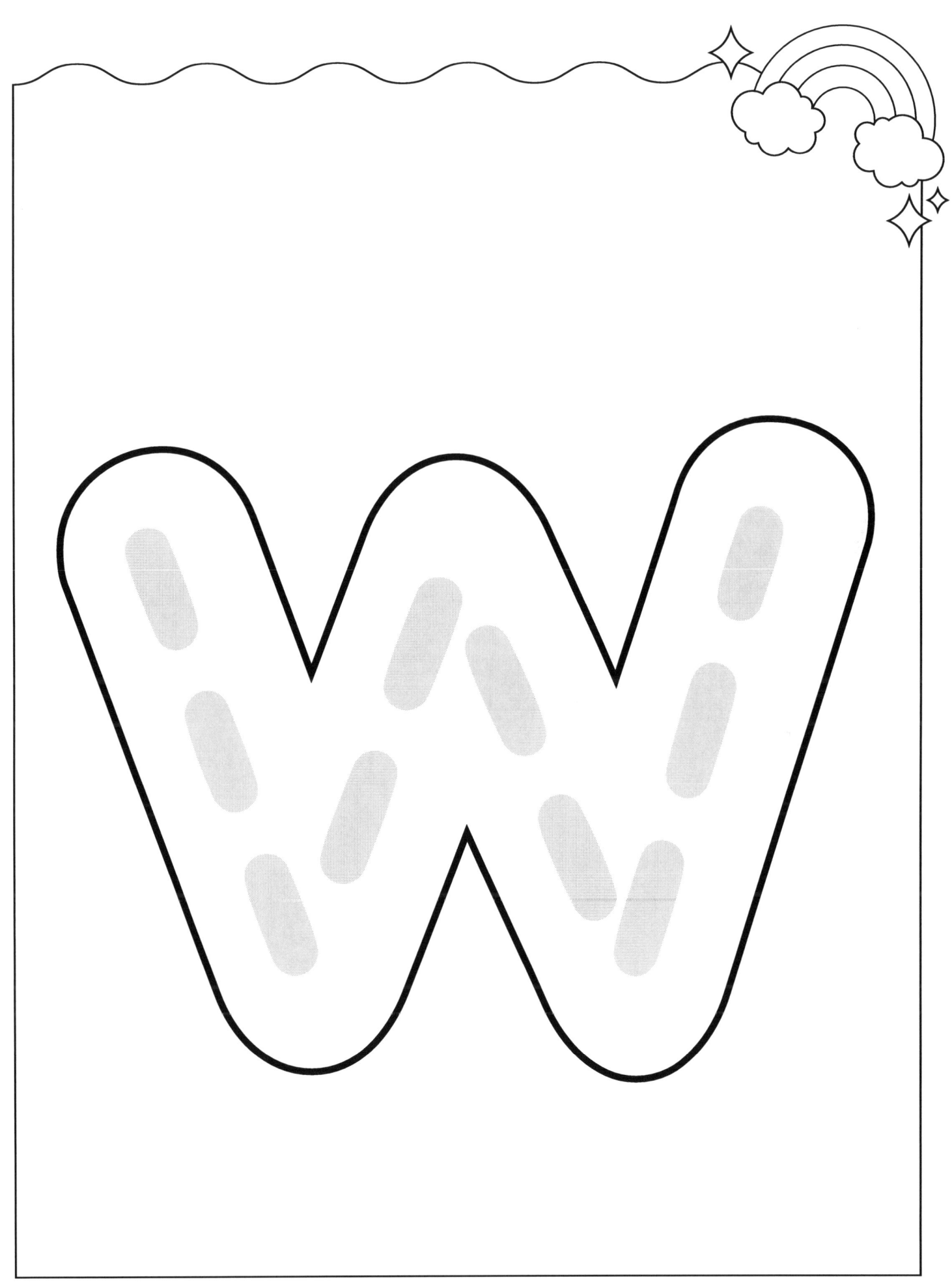

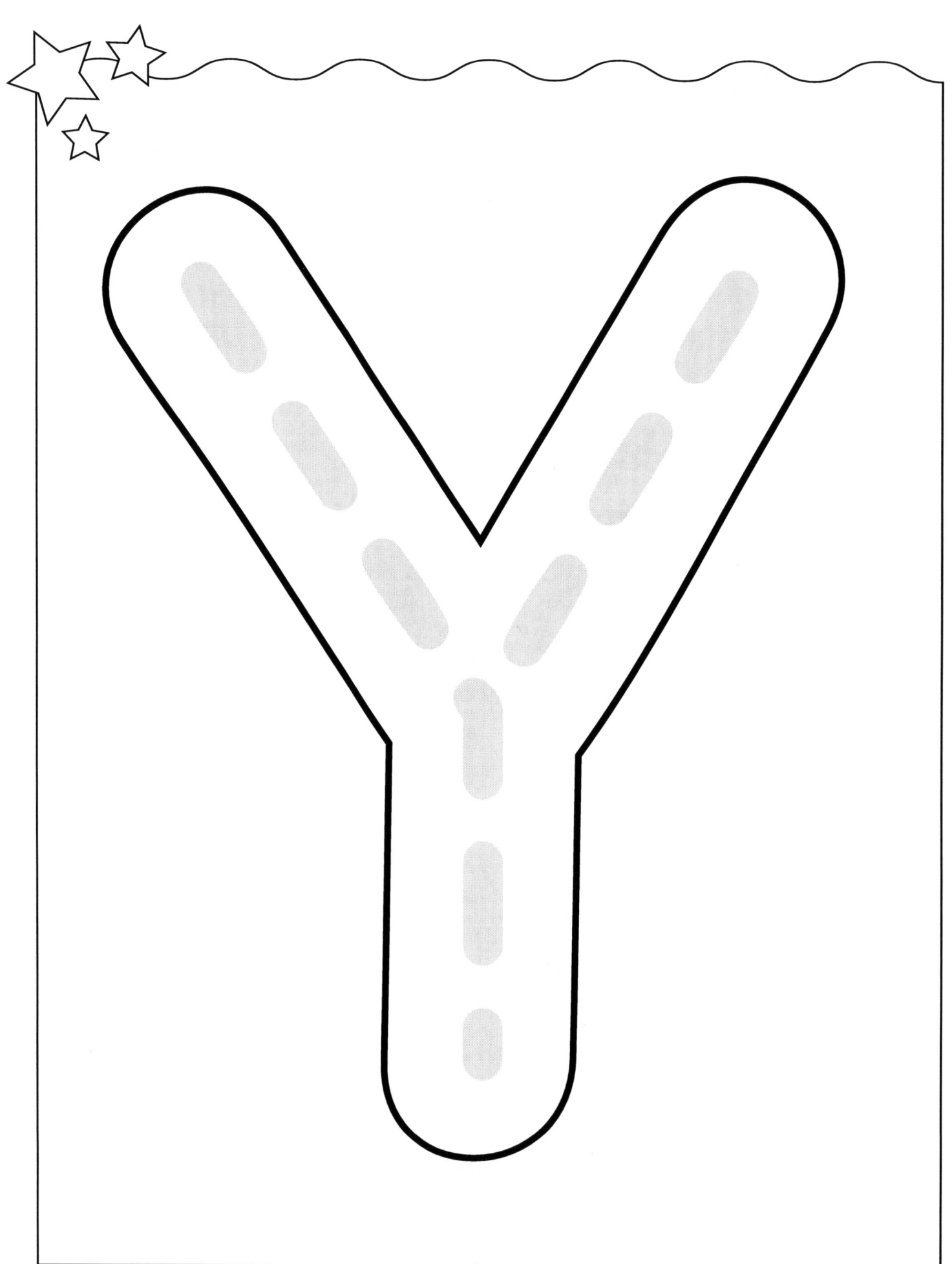

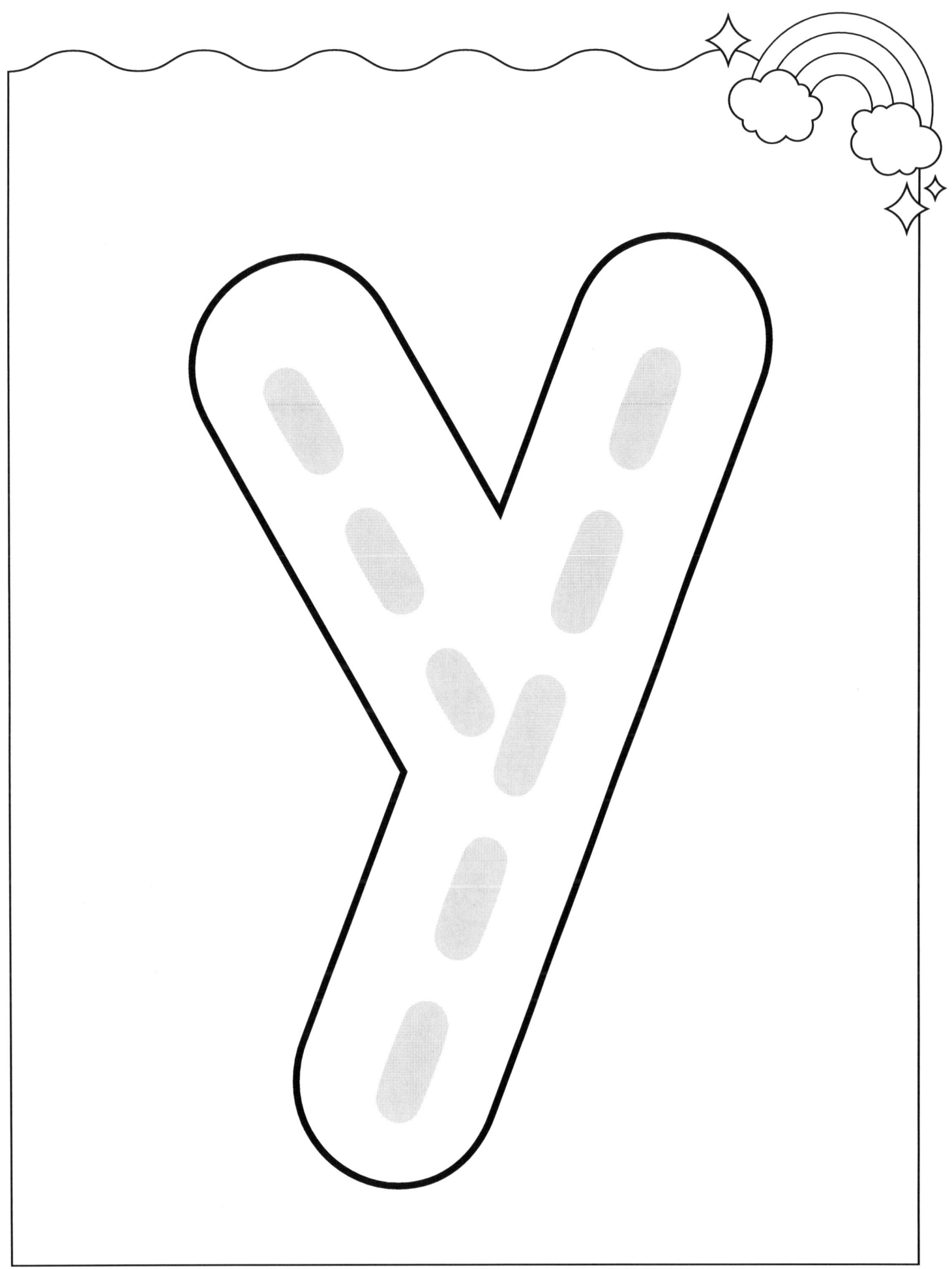

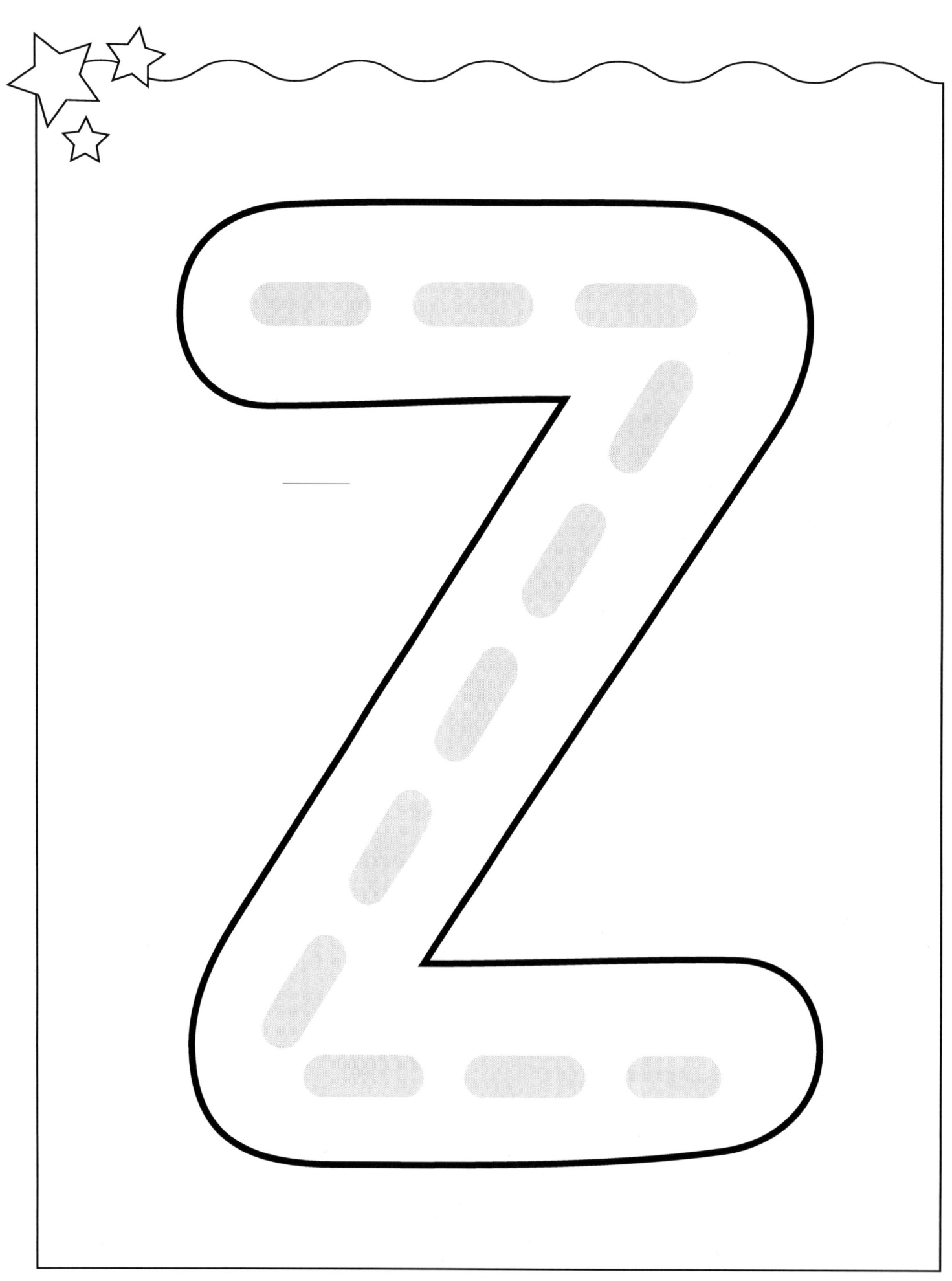

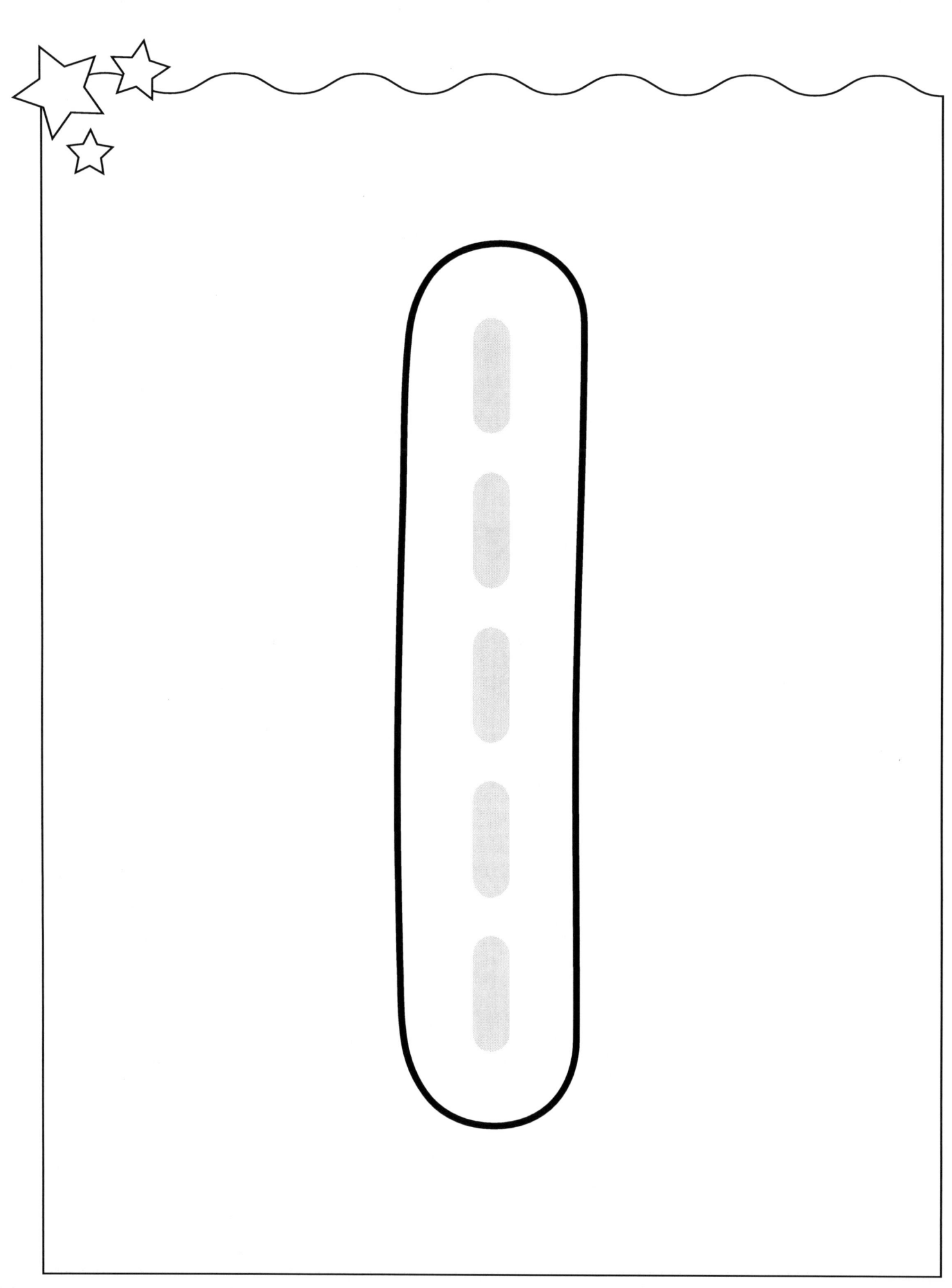

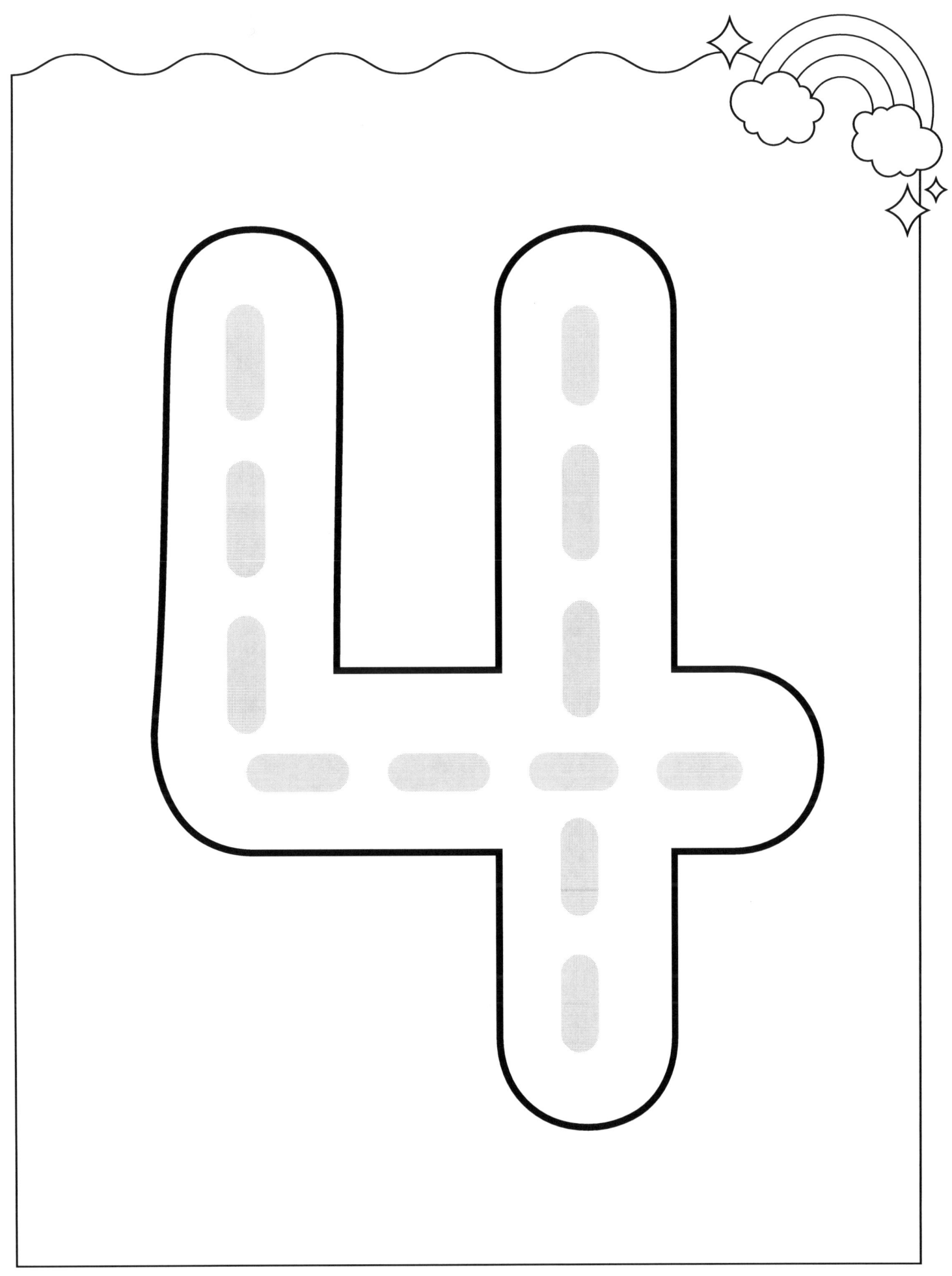

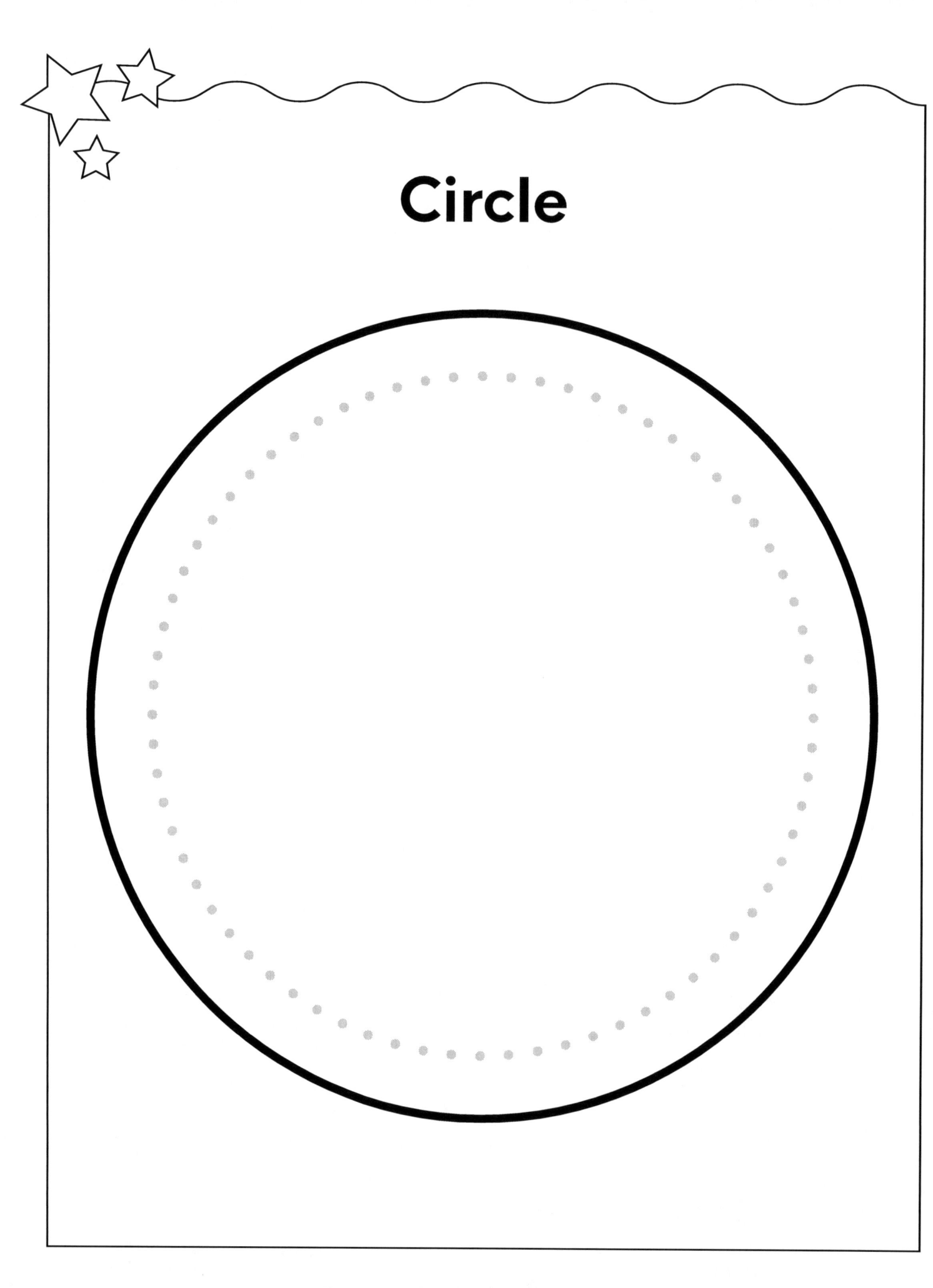

Square

Triangle

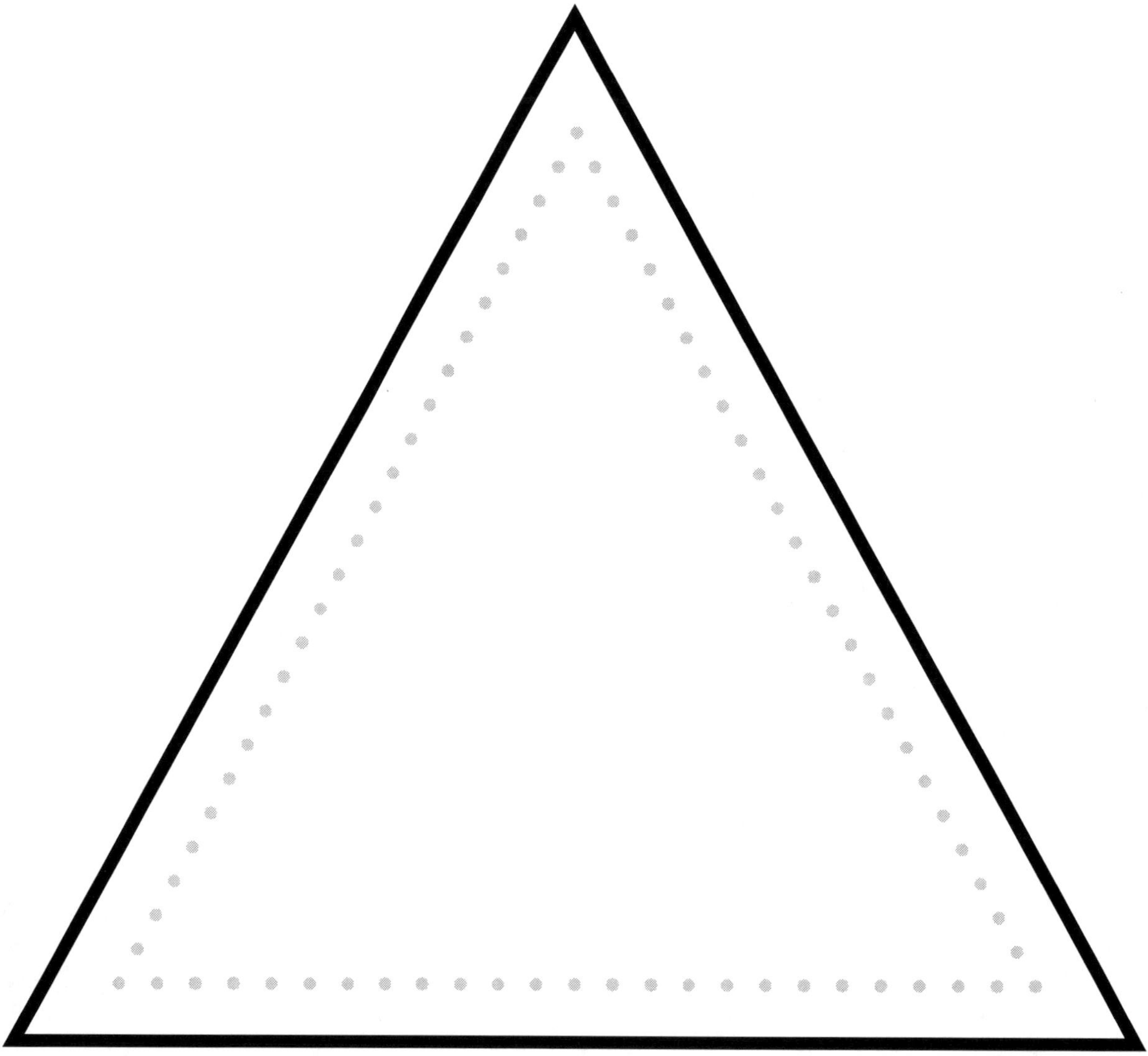

Rectangle

Pentagon

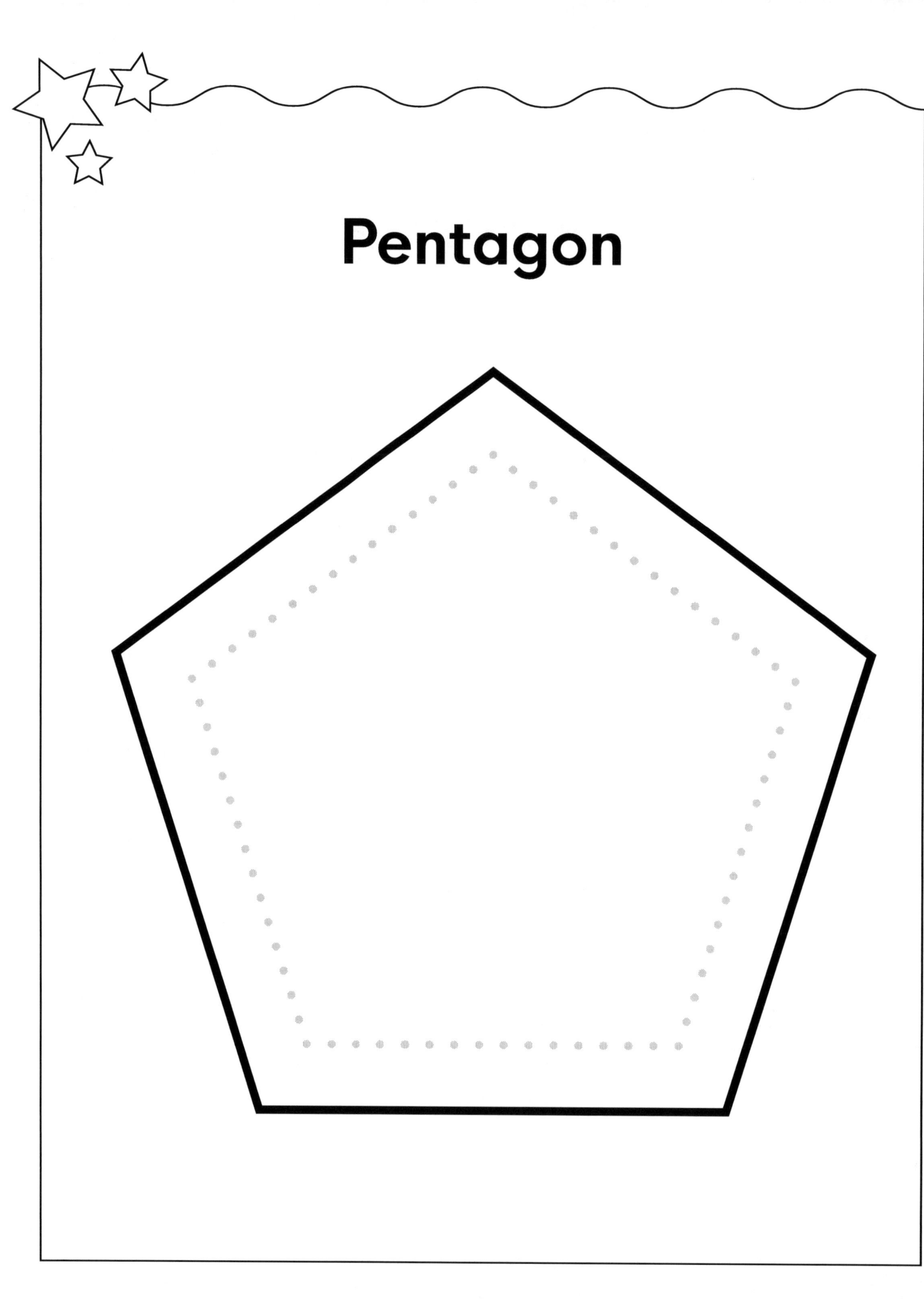

Diamond

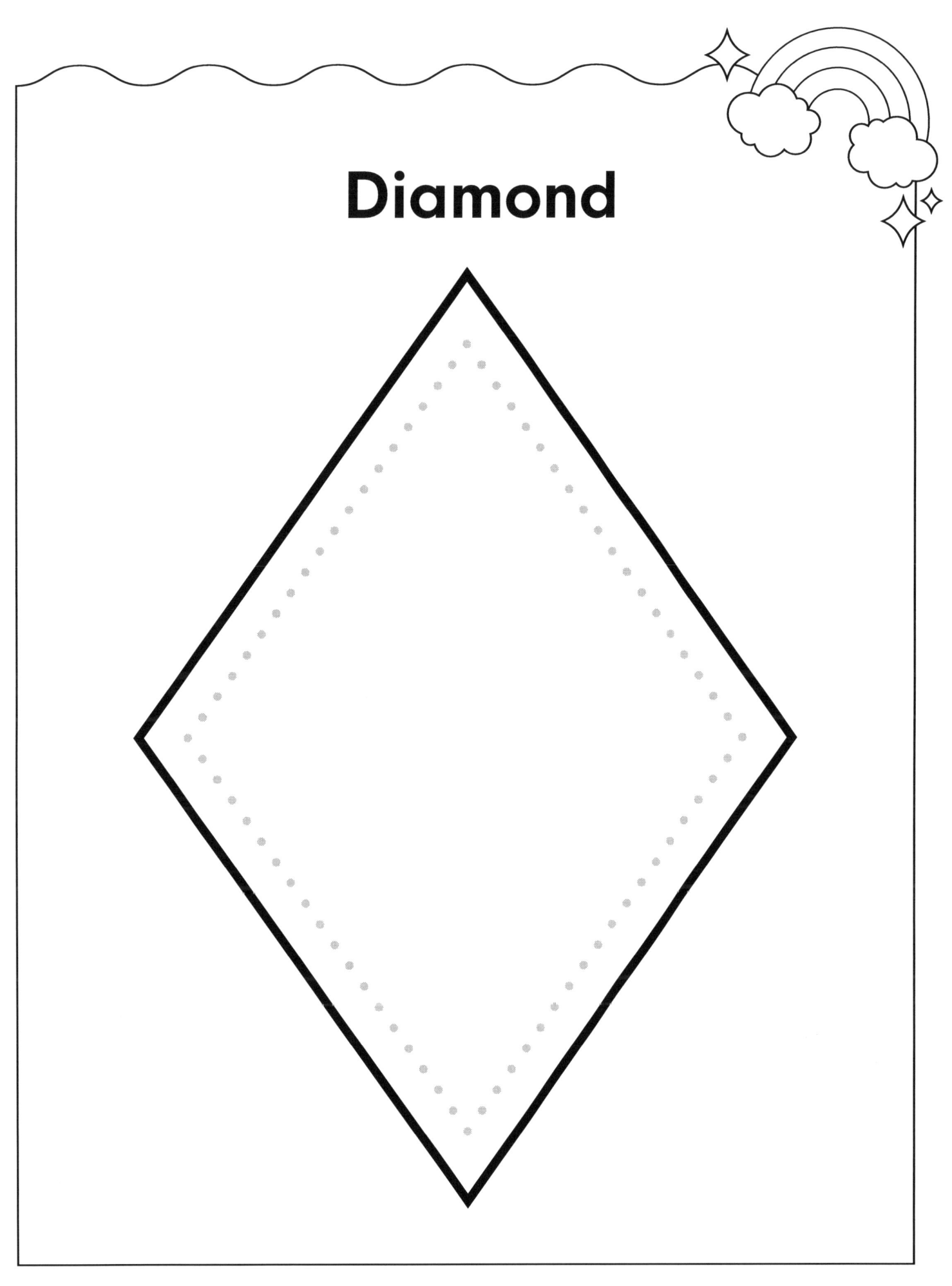

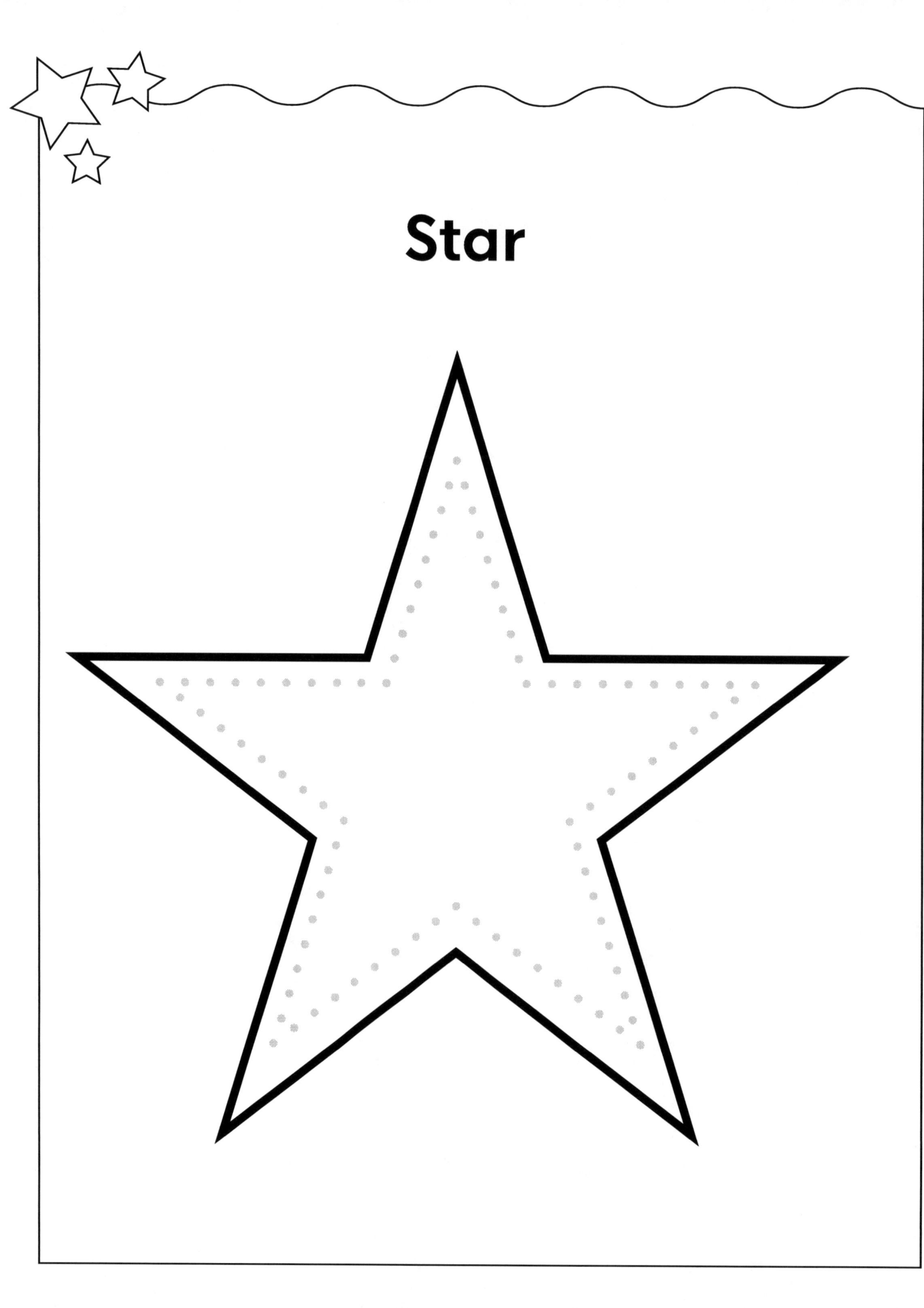

Crescent

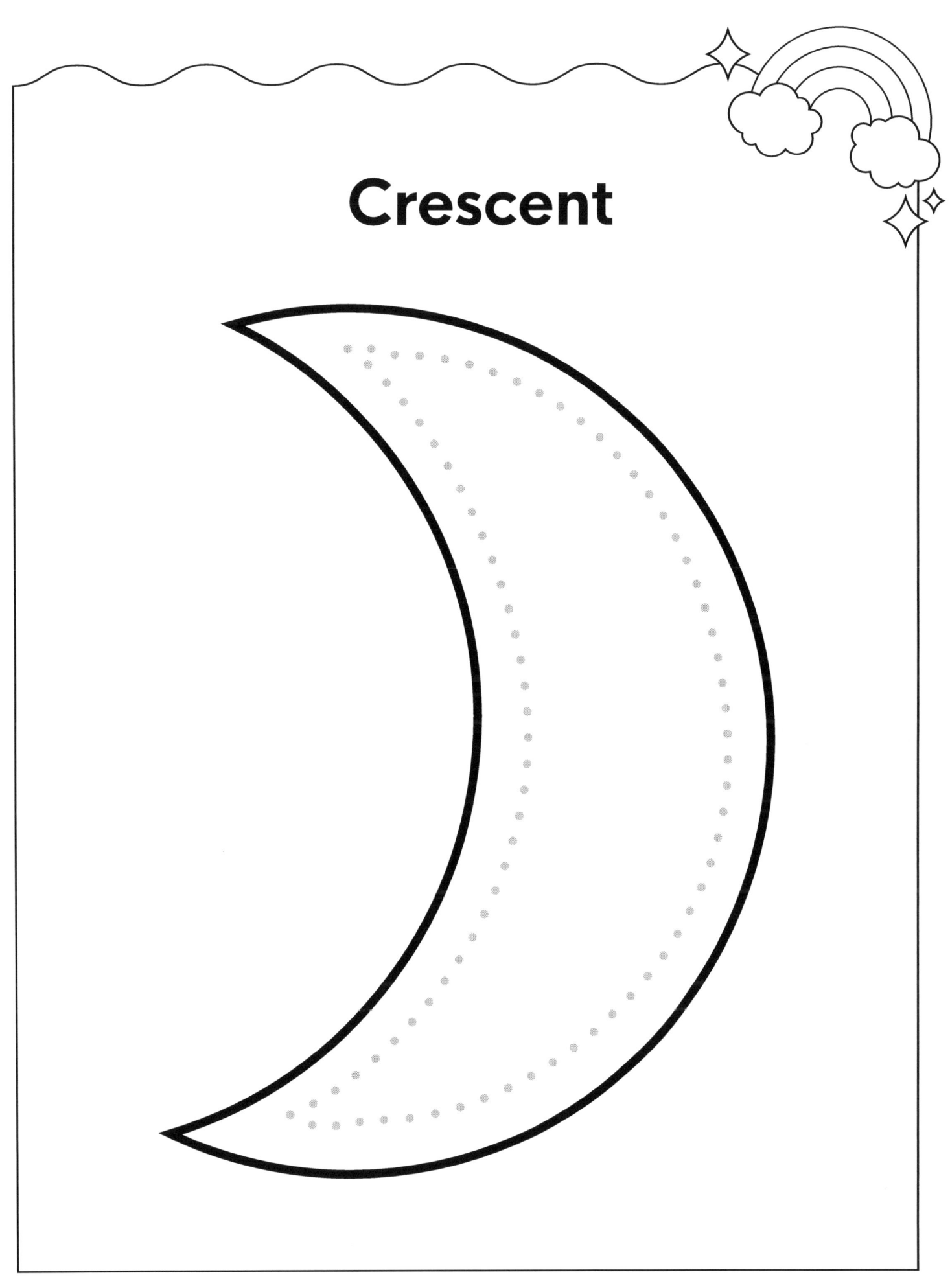

Heart

Circles

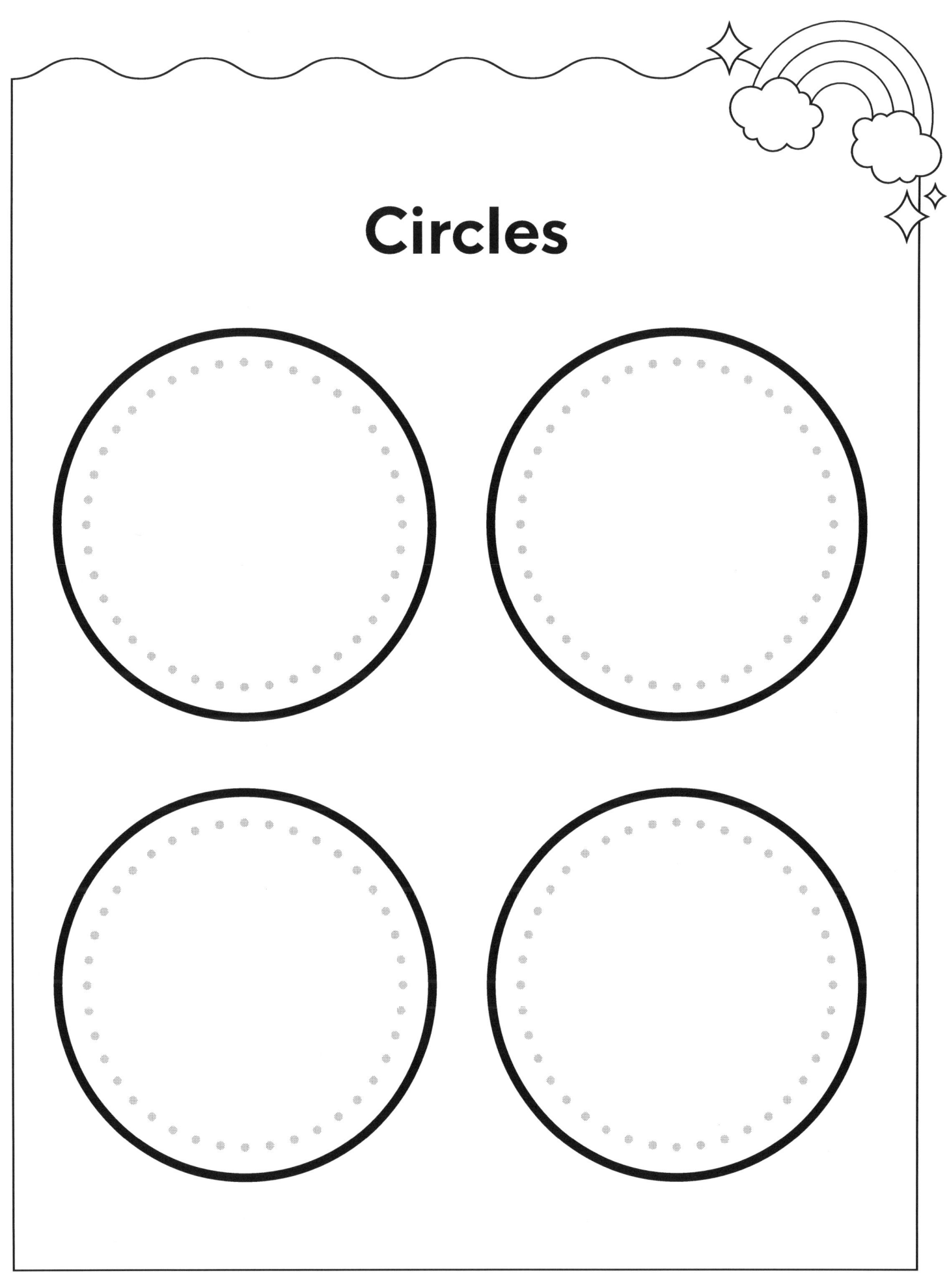

Check out these titles and more at
WWW.MODERNKIDPRESS.COM